DESIGNING INTERIOR ENVIRONMENT

DESIGNING

HBJ

HARCOURT BRACE JOVANOVICH, INC

New York   Chicago   San Francisco   Atlanta

NTERIOR ENVIRONMENT

MARY JEAN ALEXANDER

Formerly, Parsons School of Design and Pratt Institute,
and Chairman, National Committee on Education, AID

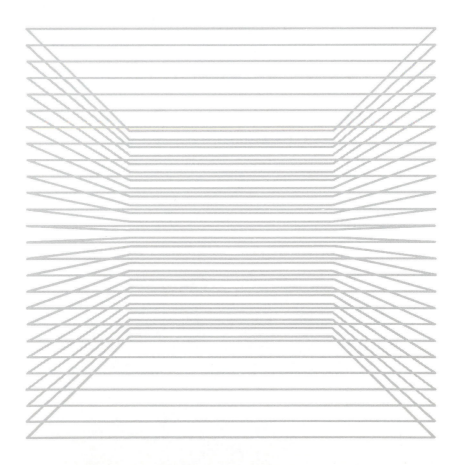

ISBN: 0-15-517372-3

Library of Congress Catalog Card Number: 77-187041

Printed in the United States of America

FOREWORD

Although a field of work that is very old indeed, interior design as practiced today is a new profession, very different from what it was only thirty-five years ago, when it still concerned itself mainly with the superficial aspects of home decoration. Even the name has changed (from the "interior decoration" of past decades), reflecting the fact that it has become a profession concerned with all areas of interior environment.

This profession of interior design is today recognized as having great importance in the conception of the whole building. Owners, architects, and designers all agree that the plan, the interior, the exterior—the entire building—must be integrated, and that interior design must be given careful attention at the earliest planning stages.

The second half of the twentieth century has seen an increase in the variety of clients seeking the services of the interior designer. The problems involved in the design of office buildings, hotels, factories, hospitals and laboratories, schools and colleges are complex. To solve these problems competently and imaginatively, today's interior designer should have familiarity with many areas. Although the aim of educators in this field is to train technically competent designers, they recognize the need for further knowledge—of history and economics and of the social forces at work in society. Such an overall training program in design and in the humanities will produce a professional who can visualize a room or a building whole. Such a designer must work with the architect in determining the needs of the people who will use the building, and in planning the relationship of rooms and spaces. He will be equipped to develop within a space an atmosphere, a way of life for people, for ultimately he is dealing with the arts and techniques of living.

In this book Mary Jean Alexander has provided a fine tool for students seeking to understand the requirements of their profession. It will make them aware of the research and work necessary to master the many areas of design involved in the creation of a functional and beautiful space.

Contemporary design is the result

of a long historical process of adopting, discarding, and adopting again the elements of design as they fulfill the needs of each era. So that the student may recognize this, Mrs. Alexander has drawn a brief picture of its history.

Her thorough and systematic explanation of the planning process is unique in the field and offers the student information that is indispensable to the successful solution of interior design problems. This treatment of the planning process, together with the many chapters on new materials and technical developments—all clearly and directly presented—must prove of inestimable value to the interior design student and instructor.

ELEANOR PEPPER
Associate/AIA

PREFACE

There is considerable confusion today concerning the training and role of the interior designer. Architects must be licensed, and training for architecture has long been standardized at a high level. Training for interior design has been haphazard and totally unstandardized. Interior design—still called "decoration" in some schools—is often taught by mail and in two- and three-year courses, some of which do not require a high-school diploma. Increasingly, however, the subject is offered within a degree program, as an elective or as a major in the department of art, design, architecture, or home economics. It is often difficult to recognize that some of these courses deal with the same subject.

The widely divergent methods of teaching and the often controversial (and overly technical) character of journals and books make a broad-based text in the field essential. *Designing Interior Environment* is intended to be a text primarily presenting principles—to enable it to be useful as a supplement in courses such as drafting or drawing, in programs in which the subject is taught

from different standpoints in more than one department, and where the subject is taught as a complete and unified course. Thus, students with differing interests will find it helpful whether they are dealing with a residential interior of traditional design or wrestling with problems of public or institutional interiors. The organization of the book is essentially developmental: historical background preceding basic principles, then the application of principles, and finally, the materials and processes available.

Chapter 4, unique in design texts, offers a step-by-step presentation of the "planning process," from programing to the final plans, perspective drawings, or models.

The chapters on materials provide sound bases for evaluating products —a vital element in the practice of design today. Because of the innovative and rapidly changing character of current chair design and manufacture, seating is given special emphasis in the chapter devoted to furniture. A separate chapter on the dwelling is aimed to meet the needs of the many students whose focus will be primarily on residential design. The future, in terms of potential and trends, is dealt with in the epilogue, and the appendix includes suggestions concerning professional procedure and business practice.

My thanks go to Richard Coats, whose knowledge of the Bauhaus school and architectural design since the Second World War led me into research that has enhanced this book. He also introduced me to the architectural schematic approach to environmental design, an approach that he develops in the house and office designs presented in Chapter 4. Suggestions from Gibson A. Danes brought me to a realization of the urgent need for expert design for mass production and, consequently, to a recognition of the changing role of the interior designer in decades to come.

Robert L. Alexander, of the Department of Art at the University of Iowa, gave me much appreciated encouragement; Harlan Sifford, also of the University of Iowa, was most helpful in my research; and Faber Birren, the authority for much of the material on color, was an interested and helpful contributor. Eleanor Pepper gave invaluable and expert assistance in checking the manuscript; Sergei Marketan provided much information on lighting; and Umberto Marcucci read the manuscript and made constructive suggestions.

My gratitude goes to my editor, Philip Ressner, and to my copyeditor, Linda Reiman, whose objectivity and proficiency made the editing process a valuable experience and contributed much to the making of this book. The enthusiasm and skill of designers Meyer Miller and Eva Bessenyey and art editors Elizabeth Early and Beth Bird, have also added greatly to the usefulness and appearance of the book.

MARY JEAN ALEXANDER

CONTENTS

INTRODUCTION

The value of a space is not the product of its function
but of its atmosphere. . . .

A space is not simply created by protecting a void from
the weather.

A factory is not a shelter for machines but a place for
man to work in.

A sacred building is to inspire man, not God!

We manipulate our environment with everything we make;
we are not responsible for its functions, but essentially
for its quality.

The whole point of "function" is to create spaces that
reflect the dignity of man.

ESKO LEHESMAA

Space is a precious resource, to be treated thoughtfully and with care and respect. In earlier days it was treated as a by-product of the organization of enclosing solids. Today space can be given its rightful meaning and significance in a structure, equal in importance to the solids. Frank Lloyd Wright considered space intrinsic to an interior—the resource that provided for human use, the life that would go on within it. This very basic concern for the human use of space is still too often ignored in the designing of interiors.

The growing interest in interior environment of the past forty years has brought the interior designer to a point where he is deeply concerned with the many complicated problems that arise in creating spaces that satisfy equally the functional, esthetic, and even the spiritual needs of man. In planning an interior environment, a person will relate to the space in which he spends his time. The ability to anticipate this is related to one's own sensitivity to surroundings, and as the young designer moves through each day, he should look and see, developing his awareness of everything he is exposed to—spaces, buildings, objects—particularly as they relate to people. Such awareness is not instinctive; the eye needs to be trained to look at and for certain elements in answer to such questions as: How does each space or object in it fulfill its esthetic or functional purpose? Is it satisfying to see? What influences are reflected? What kind of human reactions does it logically elicit? Why does one space or building delight, another bore, and still another go completely unnoticed? What is there that should be admired or criticized?

Students are often unaware of design as it affects their own environment. Many do not even realize that it is possible to control and improve their surroundings. Consciously controlled attention, supplemented by subconscious awareness, develops a kind of perception in a designer that can help him understand his surroundings as design and realize their potential as environment. It can also encourage a student to strive for original solutions to design problems rather than settle for the tried and true ones. Lewis Mumford derived much of his architectural knowledge from walks around New York City, looking, seeing, being aware of the life around him. In his "ideal scheme of education, this mode of seeing and knowing must both pervade and supplement the knowledge we receive from books, statistics and computers."

For many beginning students of design, the subject exists in a vacuum and is not clearly associated with human history. Tracing the evolution of design concepts through the development of architecture can provide a background that will give these concepts a significance that makes them truly understandable. Although designers sometimes see in the study of the history of architecture a danger of encouraging copying and imitation, Henry-Russell Hitchcock has pointed out that architecture as studied today, rather than leading to imitation, seems to "inspire a yearning to rival in originality the great ages of the past."

Today's variety of architecture relies heavily on technology, which, shortening the gap between scientific discovery and its application, increases the pace of change. Technology can provide instruments for solving a multitude of problems; the new storage and retrieval systems, for example, can put at a designer's fingertips countless specifics, such as the fatigue factors and distraction effects of shapes and colors under certain conditions. But this rapid pace of change has made it urgent that we be aware of the dangers as well as the advantages. If change is to mean progress we must evaluate it in relation to human values.

During the twenties and almost until the Second World War, architecture and technology were progressing at a more rapid pace than interior decoration or design. Engineers began to develop a new approach toward their role in creating environments, producing factory-fabricated, specialized units composed of various elements. This diminished the architect's flexibility, compelling him to deal in terms of these prefabricated units rather than in basic materials. During this period, decorators made a superficial attempt to come to terms with the machine. They used streamlining and much glass and steel, sometimes combining austere modern design with irrelevant decoration. Most of them did not understand technology, and there remained a strong dependence on the past. In the late thirties, interior design had clearly begun to evolve from interior decoration, and after the Second World War, it moved toward becoming a genuine profession.

Architects, engineers, and industrial designers, in their development of materials and new applications for old materials, are drastically changing our environment. The more building there is, the more environment is altered—for better or worse, and it is essential that the interior designer's role be as fundamental to these changes as that of the architect. There has never been greater opportunity for the interior designer. Since the Renaissance, the direction has generally been forward, toward better and more appropriate design for environment in a changing world. But if possibilities are to be realized, enlightened attitudes on the part of interior designers are required. Some merchandising practices related to sales and marketing have had a detrimental effect on the profession. One of the greatest deterrents to sound design has been the planned obsolescence that demands new lines of products at frequent intervals. This practice cheapens materials and workmanship and destroys the integrity of design, both functionally and esthetically.

If the interior designer is to take his place in the field of environmental planning, he must not only be in command of the information embodied in a comprehensive educational program, but must also be professionally rather than commercially oriented. In order to cope with new demands, new methods and materials, and the complex needs of a rapidly changing world, interior designers are beginning to broaden their goals and raise their standards of training. Training for interior design today has aims very different from those offered the finest interior decorator not many years ago. With the other designers of environment, the interior designer must aim at understanding human needs and must utilize every idea, resource, and potential to achieve a satisfactory use of interior space for all purposes and all human beings.

1

To develop a satisfactory interior environment in which to live, work, and play comfortably, it is necessary to design it with care on the basis of knowledge and sound principles. Unprecedented techniques of living, a continuously increasing body of technological knowledge, and changing social values have created new and complicated needs and have imposed a drastically swifter tempo on our mode of living.

As interior decorating evolved in this country, it was concerned only with the home. Since the Second World War, interior design has been developing. Today it is a genuine profession and interior designers are collaborating in the design of every kind of interior, from factory to specialty shop.

TRADITIONAL DESIGN: DECORATING AN ENCLOSURE

Interior decoration as practiced in this country began in the late nineteenth century. Referring to the situation in 1897, Edith Wharton wrote: "the architects of that day looked down on house decoration as a branch of dressmaking, and left the field to the upholsterers, who crammed every room with curtains, lambrequins, jardinieres of artificial plants, wobbly velvet covered tables littered with silver gew-gaws and festoons of lace on mantel pieces and dressing tables." [1] Miss Wharton became involved in the matter because she was dissatisfied with her own home and was convinced that architecture and decoration could be rescued from its "labyrinth of dubious eclecticism" (Fig. 1–1) by utilizing the experience of the past. Her book *The Decoration of Houses* helped develop an interest in interior decoration and helped determine its direction at the time—a return to eighteenth-century architectural design and standards.

In America at that time the Goulds, Vanderbilts, Morgans, and others of great wealth spent fortunes on entire rooms and furnishings taken

1. Edith Wharton, *A Backward Glance* (New York: Scribner's, 1933), p. 106.

INTERIOR DESIGN:

AN OVERVIEW

from châteaux and villas of Europe and installed in their pseudo-châteaux and villas. People of lesser wealth did the same thing on a smaller scale, and the traditional styles of Europe were considered the finest by those who had enough money to improve their homes.

Such practices required a certain amount of expertise in selection and

1–1 Typical front parlor of a late nineteenth-century home, showing the clutter characterized by Edith Wharton as "dubious eclecticism."

1–2   Dining room of Elsie de Wolfe's home before (*above*) and after (*below*) redecoration according to the new principles she advocated.

installation, and, of the pioneers in this field, Elsie de Wolfe was one of the best known. In her book *The House in Good Taste*, published in 1913, she expressed pleasure at the prospect of "simple houses with fireplaces that draw, electric lights in the proper places, comfortable and sensible furniture and not a gilt-edged, spindle-shanked table anywhere."[2] Miss de Wolfe helped to make well-to-do Americans aware of the need for more comfort, convenience, and traditional beauty in their homes (Fig. 1–2). Others, combining taste with a knowledge of color and a background of period furniture, began to offer a similar service, which was generally done without charge in connection with the sale of furnishings, on which they made their profit. Thus, interior decoration started as a casually specialized service provided through merchandising. Homeowners who did not have vast fortunes, but simply comfortable homes, also became interested in improving them and consulted the new specialists. At that time the main responsibilities of interior decorators were to plan the arrangement of existing interiors and to assist in the selection of furniture, curtains, rugs, upholstery, fabrics, and accessories: they did little designing as such.

With a greater variety of home furnishings available, the responsibilities of the decorators increased. At the close of the First World War Frank Alvah Parsons began to offer training in interior decoration at his School of Fine and Applied Art.

The contribution of these early practitioners was a real one: Edith

2. Elsie de Wolfe, *The House in Good Taste* (New York: Century House, 1913), p. 16.

Wharton struck a major blow against the chaotic, late-Victorian, overdecorated interiors; Elsie de Wolfe stood for suitability, simplicity, and proportion; and Frank Alvah Parsons provided standards of training for his students, who were given a foundation in traditional architecture and furnishings and instruction in principles of design and their application.

In 1914 a group of interior decorators in New York City organized with the aims of raising both standards of design training and the ethics of the profession. By 1931 a national group had been organized with aims similar to those of the New York group.

"MODERN" DESIGN: MANIPULATING SPACE

At the same time that these interior decorators were helping homemakers to arrange and embellish their homes on the basis of traditional ideas of design, a modern movement was developing in the field of architecture in reaction to the dependence on the past for design inspiration. This new, rebellious philosophy started toward the close of the nineteenth century with men like Louis Sullivan, and was given further impetus in the early twentieth century in the United States by Sullivan and others, such as Frank Lloyd Wright and, in Europe, by the architects of the Bauhaus and by Le Corbusier. Concerned with living in a modern industrial world, they began to develop new concepts for the design of environment. For the first time since the Renaissance, a strong, new movement developed in architecture based on a new concept of space, the use of new materials, and the thesis that architecture must be organic, must have functional integrity. The style (see Fig. 2–12) that resulted—much of it unadorned—was frighteningly unfamiliar and revolutionary for the average American, who, steeped in traditional styles, neither liked nor understood it. These efforts to create a new environment adapted to contemporary needs were similar to corresponding efforts in the past—for example, when the late-twelfth- and early-thirteenth-century builders produced the Gothic cathedrals of the then church-dominated world.

In the nineteen twenties, thirties, and forties, both styles—traditional and "modern"—were in use. The older one treated an interior as a room, a receptacle for things, to be furnished and decorated; in the newer style, a main consideration was how to use space functionally and esthetically. Until the late nineteenth and early twentieth centuries interior space had been incidental to the structure that contained it; in this new concept space was equally important in the design. This idea, not actually new, was described by the oriental philosopher Lao Tse in the sixth century B.C.:

We turn clay to make a vessel; but it is on the space where there is nothing that the utility of the vessel depends. We pierce doors and windows to make a house; but it is on these spaces where there is nothing that the utility of the house depends. Therefore, just as we take advantage of what is, we should recognize the utility of what is not.[3]

Architects began to design structures on the basis of manipulating space, so that the surrounding solids now were determined by the solution to spatial problems, and the structure became a composition of enclosure and openness.

This conception encouraged more freedom of planning. In the past a room had been bounded by walls, doors, and windows; under the new thinking, walls are no longer punched through for access or light, but become space-definers to be walked around or eliminated. Solid walls are replaced by floor-to-ceiling glass walls, doors, and windows, and by partitions that do not reach to the ceiling, which is often opened up with skylights. In this sense space extends in all directions and is defined or measured by the form that contains it

1–3 View of contemporary home, in which spaces are loosely defined.

3. Lao Tse, quoted in John Peter, *Masters of Modern Architecture* (New York: George Braziller, 1958), p. 13.

(Fig. 1–3). It can be given varieties of
expression—static or mobile, flowing
around a corner, unfolding, opening
or closing. It cannot be seen, but it
can be sensed, and with its greater
freedom and flexibility, this conception seemed the best on which to
base a contemporary design.

TODAY: TECHNOLOGY AND A NEW ECLECTICISM

Although many architects accepted
this new design concept, most interior decorators neither understood
nor approved of it. They continued to
think of their role in terms of a room,
with walls, doors, windows, and architectural elements, to be made comfortable and decorated appropriately.
As the discipline has advanced, interior designers have come to apply
this concept and other new theories
in their design. The long-standing
gulf between the so-called traditional-
ists and the proponents of modern
design is disappearing, partly due to
increased collaboration between architect and interior designer; design has
moved ahead, and contemporary- and
tradition-oriented designers, borrow-
ing from one another, have moved
closer together. Today's designer is
likely to be eclectic in his solutions
(Fig. 1–4). The success or failure of

a design does not depend on the period or style, but on whether the results successfully solve the problem. With its different needs and philosophy, the stylistic *approach* of one day can rarely be adapted to another; but the interior designer can freely use ideas, objects, and furnishings of the past when they are appropriate to his design.

The change that has resulted from this cooperation between traditional and modern designers took place over several decades. Change today is more revolutionary than evolutionary. Since the Second World War, when industry became free to direct its efforts toward nonmilitary markets, the rate of change has been increasing dizzyingly. With so much change based on an expanding technology, human and esthetic values tend to be overlooked in an overwhelming emphasis on function and quantity.

Lewis Mumford has taken the view that the "exaltation of technology" [4] places everyone in danger of being submerged by the inhuman in our developing environment. Interior designers are becoming involved in evaluating such forces and are directing their efforts toward creating the kind of progress that strikes a balance between science and human needs. Progress in architecture exists, according to Frank Lloyd Wright, only if it "creates according to the *nature of man* and his circumstances as they *both* change [emphasis added—Au.]." [5] Gropius considers architecture and environment as continuously changing, without any finality, but

also that it must create an original expression of the *needs of the human life* of its own times, "thus renewing the human spirit." [6]

Interior designers, heeding such admonitions, are coming to offer constructive guidance in helping to make sure that change is not, as Frank Lloyd Wright observed, based on "mechanized mediocracy," but the result of an "enlightened mind" rather than a "conditioned one." [7]

The present-day function of the interior designer, according to the *Dictionary of Occupational Titles*, is as follows:

Plans and designs artistic interiors for homes, hotels, ships, commercial and institutional structures and other establishments. Analyzes functional requirements, moods and purpose of furnishing interior, based on client's needs and preferences. Devises harmonious color scheme and sketches plans of rooms showing arrangement of furniture and accessories. Estimates cost and amount of materials required and presents plans to client for approval. Selects and purchases decorative and functional materials and accessories, such as furniture, lighting fixtures and pictures, or creates original designs for furnishings to conform with decorative scheme. Directs workers painting walls, laying carpets, installing fixtures and arranging furniture and accessories in position.[8]

Although the definition may be somewhat arbitrary, it is significant that it has much in common with

4. Lewis Mumford, "Architecture As a Home for Man," *Architectural Record* (February 1968), p. 113.

5. Frank Lloyd Wright, *The Architecture of Democracy*, four lectures given at the Royal Institute of British Architects, May 1969.

6. Walter Gropius, *Scope of Total Architecture* (New York: Harper & Row, 1955), p. 43.

7. Frank Lloyd Wright, *Future of Architecture* (New York: Horizon Press, 1953), p. 325.

8. *Dictionary of Occupational Titles*, U.S. Department of Labor, Manpower Administration, Bureau of Employment Security, 1965.

the definition of an architect. Essentially the definitions imply greater emphasis on esthetics for the interior designer and on the technical for the architect. While this is true, the tendency now is for the two to move closer together, with architects receiving more training in esthetic aspects and interior designers learning more about technical matters. In fact, during the past few years many areas traditionally those of either architect or interior designer have come to overlap, and there is a common aim—creation of a satisfactory environment for human use. The main difference is that architects are concerned with exterior as well as interior space. Their shared, broad aim not only embraces the appearance and purpose of the environment, and relies on science and technology, but also includes a concern for sociological values. Today's interior specialist, then, must be able to organize into a functioning and attractive whole, the spatial, visual, sociological, physical, and psychological aspects of an interior.

The recent rapid increase in population and a vastly expanded variety of products are having an emphatic effect on interior design. Where, in the past, it was generally considered that what was excellent was rare, this no longer need be the case. The need for excellence of design that accommodates itself to mass production offers new opportunities to the specialist, whether he is designing interiors, furniture, wall coverings, carpets, textiles, or incidental furnishings. The craftsman is disappearing as economically unfeasible; good designers qualified to design and to select products on a qualitative basis are greatly needed.

BIBLIOGRAPHY

BATTERSBY, MARTIN. *The Decorative Twenties* (Walker, 1970). Thorough coverage of decoration, art, and design during a period that was more than slightly chaotic.

CASSON, HUGH. *Inscape* (Architectural Press, 1968). Contributions by seven British authorities on architecture and interior design. Includes a factual discussion—"The Education of the Interior Designer"—by Misha Black. Many good illustrations.

FELDMAN, E. B. *Art as Image and Idea* (Prentice-Hall, 1967). Art as part of environment. Comprehensive; a valuable reference book. Many illustrations coordinated well with the text.

GOWANS, ALAN. *Images of American Living* (Lippincott, 1964). A thoughtful, comprehensive account of architectural furnishings in the United States and their relation to the history of the country. Particularly interesting are the comments in Chapter 2 on the evolution of design for living in the twentieth century.

HUXTABLE, ADA LOUISE. *Will They Ever Finish Bruckner Boulevard?* (Macmillan, 1970). Preface by Daniel P. Moynihan. Some of the author's columns on the contemporary architectural scene from the *New York Times*. Important comments by a writer who early criticized the waste of natural and technological resources. Arranged by subject.

MC HALE, JOHN. *R. Buckminster Fuller* (George Braziller, 1962). A clear account of Fuller's work and its development, by a man who worked closely with him. Text and photographs.

ROGERS, MEYRIC R. *American Interior Design* (Bonanza, 1947). A history of interior design and decoration in the United States, with accompanying social history. Useful photographs of interiors and exteriors.

2

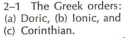

2–1 The Greek orders:
(a) Doric, (b) Ionic, and
(c) Corinthian.

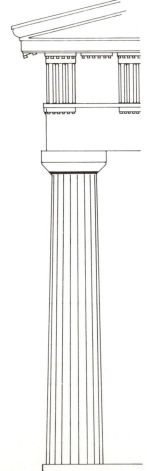

a

Although today a few tradition-smashing designers conceive of a new, unprecedented environment that can be created only after all previous design concepts have been destroyed, most serious designers, even while experimenting with what may be revolutionary ideas, continue to profit from the design of the past. Until relatively recently the history of manmade environment was mainly the history of architecture, the profession most concerned with it. Architecture provides shelter and a background for living, but it is more than that: to be architecture, a building must have esthetic merit. Thus architecture is an art, but one that differs from the arts of painting and sculpture in two ways —it is designed for use, and so must be functional; and space is basic to it. Architecture is concerned with the manipulation of three-dimensional elements, which may be interior spaces, or solids, or the exterior spaces around and between buildings. Eero Saarinen said that the purpose of architecture is "to shelter and enhance man's life on earth and to fulfill his belief in the nobility of his existence." The history of architecture is concerned with the way space has been shaped to create human environment.

THE BEGINNINGS: GREECE AND ROME

Early Western architecture reached its peak in the fifth century B.C. in Greece. It is based on post-and-lintel construction, in which a horizontal member (or lintel) spans the space between two vertical supports, usually columns (the posts). The horizontal piece developed into an entablature, which includes the architrave, frieze, and cornice—and the triangular pediment, which rests on it. By brilliantly relating the dimensions of the columns, the spaces between, and the entablature, the Greeks achieved a rhythm and a harmony of proportion, still considered outstanding, in which all parts were related to the whole according to specific rules.

Three distinct styles, known as orders, were developed (Fig. 2–1). In each, proportions were governed by

DESIGN INFLUENCES

the relationship between the diameter and the height of the column, which determined the module and provided a unit of measurement for each order. The distinguishing features of each are seen most readily in the column (base, shaft, and capital) and the entablature. The earliest order was the Doric, in which a massive, sturdy, fluted column emphasizes the support function, and the capital is undecorated. The Ionic order, dignified and graceful, less bulky, has a slender fluted shaft and a capital decorated with a spiral volute. The Corinthian order employs an even slenderer column, with a capital shaped like an inverted bell and embellished with stylized acanthus leaves. The contribution of Greek architects to human environment was somewhat limited by their almost sole concern with monumental temples. Interior space, as it accommodated man, was of little interest to them.

While Greek architecture was planned for the cultured public and appealed to the intellect, Roman architects were motivated by the need to provide meeting places for the

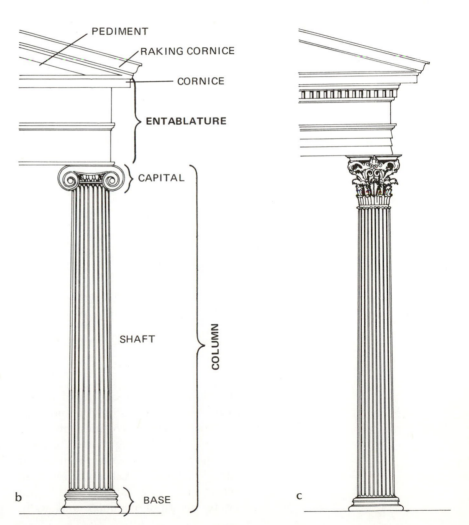

9

2–2   Interior of the Pantheon in the painting by Pannini.

varied activities of crowds of people who liked luxury, strength, and magnificence. Huge volumes of space (Fig. 2–2) were engineered for these dramatic public activities, both secular and religious. Great coliseums, circuses, and public baths, heated by hot water in pipes in floors and walls, were constructed. Triumphal arches commemorated emperors, aqueducts brought water to the cities, and fine roads facilitated the movement of soldiers and trade. The arch and vault, which had originated in Asia Minor were added to the post and lintel to create buildings such as the

Pantheon, in which the new theories were applied and new materials used: although exteriors were still of marble, concrete now became an important structural material. Palaces and privates villas were built for the pleasure and convenience of Rome's privileged classes. The houses were constructed around a courtyard, or atrium, onto which the service quarters, public rooms, and offices generally opened, while the private quarters were usually beyond, around a garden surrounded by a columned arcade. The Roman houses best known today (many with interior features preserved) used by wealthy Romans as a summer resort, are seen in the ruins at Pompeii.

By the fourth century A.D., Constantine gave Christianity imperial recognition, and during the religious upsurge that followed, many churches were built.

THE MIDDLE AGES: ROMANESQUE AND GOTHIC

The architecture called Romanesque, the first architecture that could be said to be of the Middle Ages, was based on earlier building principles, although much of the technical knowledge had been lost, including that of construction of the vault and the use of concrete. The Romanesque builders perfected the art of masonry and experimented with structural forms. In order to support a stone roof that was fireproof and more dignified than the early wooden ones, they developed a system of piers that supported a new kind of vault, a rib vault. The rib vault was perfected in the thirteenth and fourteenth centuries by the Gothic master builders,

who produced a strikingly new kind of building. The features of the Gothic style—the rib vault, flying buttress, and pointed arch—were developed to meet complex structural needs. Interior piers now supported the soaring vaults, whose lateral thrust was counterpoised by flying buttresses. Solid walls between the exterior piers were no longer necessary, and they were replaced by beautiful stained-glass windows, which permitted the interiors to be flooded with colored light.

THE RENAISSANCE

The Renaissance movement, which was to dominate architecture and environment for the next five hundred years, began in the early fifteenth century in the prosperous city of Florence, where merchant princes were amassing fortunes through trade. The first truly Renaissance building may be said to have been designed by Filippo Brunelleschi, who created a contemporary style of building that was adapted from the classical forms he had become familiar with in his study of Roman ruins. The structure that was to be most commonly used was based on the classic columns and pilasters, with an entablature and pediment sometimes added, particularly in the case of church architecture.

Where Gothic architecture had been vertical and soaring, Renaissance buildings emphasized the horizontal in their façades. Renaissance architecture is characterized by calculated simplicity, achieved through clarity of form, geometric harmony, refinement of detail, and linear outlining of the parts, which, as in Greek architecture, were often based on formulas and were beautifully proportioned to the

2–3 Alberti's Palazzo Rucellai, Florence, Italy.

Battista Alberti, who designed a three-story building with classical orders applied as an important part of the façade. The design of the façade of a building was often given primary importance during the Renaissance, sometimes to the detriment of the interior space.

BAROQUE AND ROCOCO

Toward the end of the Renaissance, reaction against the restrained classicism resulted in the Baroque period, roughly from the early sixteenth to the mid-eighteenth century. The academic rules that had governed were generally disregarded and expression was free and imaginative. The architecture was dramatic and complex, dynamic rather than static, with calculated surprises. It was planned to give an effect of infinity with apparently limitless distances and spaces flowing from an interior into a garden, park, or plaza. In a Baroque environment, many different arts were combined to create a harmonious whole, with an emphasis on curves of great variety, and a strong feeling of movement. Form and applied ornament—simulated draperies and scrolls, cherubs, and many illusionistic effects in plaster and paint—were used together with an exciting and sometimes unexpected interplay of forces (Fig. 2–4). Domestic interiors were furnished with impressive magnificence, and the visual effect was considered more important than comfort. Marble was a favorite material, and where not available, was simulated with paint on wood or plaster. Brilliant colors were popular. Most of the architects of the time were also sculp-

whole. At this time, because life was becoming more peaceful, there was less need for fortress dwellings, and Florentines began to develop an interest in the comfort and appearance of their domestic environment. One of the landmarks in this architecture—the Palazzo Rucellai (Fig. 2–3)—was the work of the great architect Leone

tors, and sculpture became an important part of design.

The Rococo, an early-eighteenth-century outgrowth of the Baroque in Italy, was similar, equally complex, but less powerful, more delicate, and smaller and lighter in scale. Ornament, such as foliage, shells, flowers, arabesques, and scrolls, was used profusely, both in architecture and on furniture, and little attempt made to relate them to the structure beneath. All geometric forms were abandoned; even circles were modified into ovals.

IN FRANCE

THE LOUIS'

In the late seventeenth and early eighteenth centuries France, under Louis XIV, became the cultural center of Europe. The arts were encouraged, and artists and craftsmen were organized and given space for their work in the Louvre, the royal palace of Paris. The Baroque style that had started in Italy was perfected in France, strongly influenced by the tastes of the king, whose main ideal was magnificence. The desire for pomp and display produced many elaborate churches and palaces, the greatest of which—at Versailles—became the model for palaces all over Europe. Large in scale, formal, and of a design more restrained than Italian Baroque, its basic lines were straight and covered by ornament. Interiors were generally majestic, pompous, elegant, and highly decorated (Fig. 2–5). Furniture was heavy, often gilded, and covered with carving in which many curved forms predominated. Walls of wood finished in a natural tone or painted white

2–4 The Villa Lechi, showing curved forms and flowing spaces typical of the Baroque.

with gold moldings were sometimes hung with tapestries. Heavy materials were used, such as damasks, brocatelles, brocades, and satins. Chairs were slightly more comfortable, and as more printed books appeared, bookcases were developed from the earlier cupboards. Colors were strong and bright—rich golds, crimsons, deep greens, and blues.

The rise of a new wealthy class during the latter part of this period brought forth a new kind of residence—smaller châteaux and country and town houses. During the Regency period, between the reigns of Louis XIV and his grandson, Louis XV, there was a gradual transition from the majestic formality of the Louis XIV court interiors to a less formal and more comfortable style.

The Rococo that had started in Italy was adapted and developed into an important style in France during the reign of Louis XV. Both the rooms and the furniture of Louis XV were much smaller in scale and decorated with informal, whimsical, romantic, and sentimental designs (Fig. 3–6). Straight lines were replaced with flowing, open, freehand curves in which subtle balance was achieved asymmetrically. Even the more formal rooms were relatively small, and intimate rooms for games, music, and conversation were planned for comfort and convenience. They were usually paneled in wood, in a natural color or painted in a soft tone with moldings of white or dull gold. Often the panels were filled with painted

decoration that was inventive and amusing. Chimney pieces of marble or wood were a prominent feature.

Most of the furniture, also designed on curved lines, was carved, some simply, some ornately, with a natural wood or painted finish. Chairs were caned or upholstered, and cabinets and writing tables were decorated with ormolu mounts. A variety of unique upholstered pieces, including the chaise longue, came into use. The curves of the furniture and architecture were combined into a beautiful rhythmic unity. Shells, ribbons, scrolls, and flowers were the basis of patterns (using curved forms) on textile, satins, velvets, damasks, brocades, and fine cottons. Mauve, soft grayed pinks, greens,

2–5 A Louis XIV interior of the Hôtel Lambert. Majestic, straight forms, heavily decorated, are characteristic.

2–6 A Louis XVI salon,
balanced and orderly.
A Louis XV chair is in the
foreground.

grays, and putty tones were combined with white or gold.

Some years before the death of Louis XV, the design of both furniture and interiors began to be more restrained, and by the time of the reign of Louis XVI design was balanced, orderly, and symmetrical, based on straight lines and controlled, simple geometric curves (Fig. 2–6). Walls were paneled, natural finish or painted, or made of plaster and painted or covered with wallpaper or fabric. Chimney pieces were decorated simply and usually made of marble. Decorative ornament was used both in architecture and on furniture and was varied, with carved or painted fluting, frets, rosettes, swags, urns, floral arrangements, pastoral scenes, and trophy panels. Furniture was no less comfortable than that of Louis XV style. Chairs were upholstered or caned, and often an oval back was combined with a square seat. Beds were smaller, with the wood frame sometimes exposed. Marble was used on table and commode tops and leather on the tops of writing tables. Toule de Jouy, cotton printed with scenes—usually pastoral and enclosed in a medallion—was popular and is still in use today. All-over conventional patterns and stripes were in demand in damasks, taffetas, and brocades, and colors were still soft—light blue or pink, green, gray, and many off-whites. Gold was still used, but less commonly.

DIRECTOIRE

In the Directoire period (1795–1804), between the time of Louis XVI and the Empire, the slender refined forms and straight lines of the Louis XVI style continued, but both rooms and furniture were simpler and more severe, with less ornamentation. The influence of the excavations at Pompeii and of the military character of the government are found in ornament—either classic motifs of antiquity, or drums, spears, stars, and trumpets. Beautifully proportioned, the design was light and graceful. Mahogany, ebony, and light fruitwoods were popular. Colors were either fresh and bright, as the red, white, and blue of the flag, or subtle —grayed golds, reds, and greens with charcoal blacks such as those found in Pompeian houses.

EMPIRE

Classic revival was in full force during Napoleon's Empire (1804–1814). Absolute symmetry was the rule, and rooms were dignified and masculine (Fig. 2–7). As Napoleon gained power, the buildings that served as a backdrop to his rise became regal, solid, grand, and pompous—designed to help promote his imperial image. Walls were usually of plaster, with painted decoration, wallpaper, or fabric stretched on the wall or hung in folds. The more important interiors had a clearly architectural character, with definite cornices, pilasters, or columns and, frequently, panels over the doors and windows. Mantels were usually of marble, and basically of

classic design—some simple, others highly ornamented.

Furniture was heavier and a little stiffer and less comfortable than during the Directoire period. Many different styles of chairs were made, both caned and upholstered. Mahogany was the most popular wood, but more furniture was painted than previously. Metal inlays were used as mounts to decorate the furniture, and decoration was based on symbols of power and war, and on Rome and Egypt—the victory wreath, torch, eagle, rosette, bee (Napoleon's personal symbol), and obelisk. Commodes and consoles with mirrored backs were popular, and color, both bold and subtle, was important: deep greens, golds, grays, mustard yellows, wine reds, blues, and purples. This period inspired both the English Regency and German Biedermeier, and its influence was felt in Italy and the United States.

French styles (described above) were essentially those of the court and city. Many, however, were adapted by craftsmen and cabinetmakers in the provinces, giving rise to the term French Provincial. This practice was started during the reign of Louis XIII in the early seventeenth century, and furniture that originated then continued to be made long after his reign. The sumptuous Louis XIV design was not readily adaptable, though. The Louis XV style, with its small scale and comfort, was very popular in the provinces and remained so long after the period had ended. Its influence accounts for a large share of the eighteenth-century provincial furniture in France. Some Louis XVI furniture was also adapted for village and country houses, but little Directoire and even less Empire furniture were adapted for this purpose.

2–7 The music room at
Malmaison, an Empire design.

2–8   A William and Mary
cabinet.

IN ENGLAND

WILLIAM AND MARY

Because William and Mary had spent most of their lives in Holland, the style that prevailed in England during their reign (1689–1702)—contemporary with Louis XIV and the Baroque on the continent—was considerably influenced by Dutch values of the time. William and Mary were home-loving and more domestic than most monarchs and the furniture shows this, being smaller and more comfortable than that of other contemporary styles. During this period, furniture designers contributed more new ideas to residential interiors than did architects. Forms were basically rectangular, with straight and curved lines in the decoration (Fig. 2–8). The highboy, slant-top secretary, knee-hole desk, several new kinds of tables, and a settee consisting of two chair backs with a simple upholstered seat were introduced. Queen Mary led the way in a movement to collect China, and every fine home had either wall brackets or a cabinet with shelves to display their collections. Walnut replaced oak as the favorite wood, and marquetry, lacquer, and wood veneers became common.

QUEEN ANNE

Although Queen Anne, whose reign was brief (1702–1714), had little interest in such matters, design of this period is exceptionally beautiful. Graceful curves dominated, pieces were smaller, and the cabriole leg (Fig. 2–9) was used widely; chair and sofa backs were higher, and small upholstered sofas appeared. A highbacked chair was introduced that had small wings to protect against drafts. China cabinets were still popular, and secretaries replaced the earlier heavy chests (Fig. 2–8). Colors were influenced by Chinese rugs and porcelains. Lacquer was widely used as a finish, and walnut and mahogany were the most popular woods. The influence of the style went far beyond 1714 and was strong enough to carry well into the Georgian period, which followed.

GEORGIAN

The Georgian period (1714–1812) covers almost a century as well as the reigns of three kings—George I, II, and III—and parallels those of Louis XV and XVI and the Empire in France. There was a decided difference between the early and the late styles. After the death of Queen Anne, the mahogany furniture began to be heavier and more ornate. Design was influenced by some of the outstanding architects, Inigo Jones and Sir Christopher Wren, for example, and classic architectural elements, such as pilasters and columns, were incorporated into furniture motifs. By the middle of the period furniture and interiors were simpler and smaller in scale. At the end of the period they had become classical and delicate, showing the Greek and Pompeian influence. Satinwood became very popular during the latter part of the period.

Chippendale

Several important designers worked in this period (Fig. 2–10). One of these was Thomas Chippendale (1718–1779), a designer and a cabinetmaker. At different times he was influenced by certain French and Chinese styles, which he adapted—

2–9 The cabriole leg seen in a typical Queen Anne chair.

usually in an original and beautiful way—in chairs, bookcases, tables, desks, sofas, beds, and clocks.

Hepplewhite

George Hepplewhite (?–1786) also represents a style, although there are no known authentic pieces of his furniture in existence. He is especially known for his chairs, which were usually smaller and more elegant than Chippendale's. His shield back is the best known of his chair backs, but he made a number of others—wheel, heart, and the Prince of Wales feathers, for example. He also made a variety of small tables, cabinets, desks, and sideboards. His furniture was usually decorated with inlay, painted motifs, or low-relief carving.

Sheraton

Thomas Sheraton (1750–1806) was a designer of furniture rather than a cabinetmaker. His designs were as elegant as Hepplewhite's and similar in scale, but he preferred straight lines to curves. He designed

2–10 Furniture in the styles of three designers prominent in the Georgian period: (a) a Chippendale table, (b) a Hepplewhite tambour writing table, (c) a Sheraton settee.

a

b

many kinds of tables and was famous for his skill in devising concealed drawers. His chair backs were usually rectangular with painted flowers, festoons, or medallions.

The Adam Brothers

The four Adam brothers (1728–1792) had a powerful influence on design. John Swarbrick says of Robert, the most famous:

He was the first architect in this country who showed how the principles of unity of effect could be applied in order to bring the accessories and appointments into accord with the architectural treatment. Too many architects had been content to provide the structure and leave the owners of the houses without any advice or guidance with regard to their equipment. No details were too insignificant to interest him. He designed furniture of all descriptions . . . carpets and gold and silver plate.[1]

Their architecture was decorated in plaster relief with graceful, delicate

1. John Swarbrick, *The Works and Architecture of Robert and John Adam* (London: Alec Tiranti, 1959), p. 1.

c

2–11 Robert Adam's Etruscan
Room at Osterley Park House,
Middlesex, England.

designs based on classical motifs, such as urns, swags, scrolls, and medallions, which were also used on the furniture (Fig. 2–11). They are not known for their chairs, but designed many cabinets, bookcases, tables, and mirrors, which were usually made in the shops of Hepplewhite or Chippendale. Under their influence the sideboard became popular. Their furniture usually had straight, tapering legs and basic rectangular forms that were relieved by some curved shapes, as in a chair seat or back, or in the ornament. The design was similar in feeling to that of the Louis XVI period. Popular colors were soft blues, grays, mauves, and yellows, used with white and a gray-green called "Adam" green, and preferred fabrics had small-scale patterns.

REGENCY

The period of the English Regency (1810–1820) covers the time during which the Prince of Wales—later (very briefly) George IV—acted as regent for his father, who had been declared insane. The style, influenced by Directoire and Empire styles in France, had its effects on design until the time of Queen Victoria. The Prince Regent loved extravagance, and the artificiality of the social background was reflected in the design of the time, which ran from very fine to very bad. Walls were mainly plaster, with many pilasters and pediments, usually in a color contrasting with the background, providing strong value contrasts and silhouettes that emphasized the design. Light earthtones or soft greens against rich browns and deep greens, as well as black with gold dominated. There were comfortable upholstered pieces, and a variety of tables (Fig. 2–12),

many with a tripod or pedestal base. Classical ornamental detail, often in ormolu or brass, ebony, and lacquer were common, as were all-over leaf and flower patterns in carpets. Windows were hung with elaborate curtains of velvets, satins, and damasks in brilliant colors with many swags and much fringe. Stripes were popular.

VICTORIAN

The Victorian period (1837–1901) produced no genuine style. There were many movements, but no strong leadership, and Queen Victoria had little interest in design. The early designs were adapted from the Regency style, but in such a way as to be scarcely recognizable; later designs were adapted from the Turkish, Gothic, Venetian, and Egyptian. Chairs had fairly low seats and high backs. Upholstery was tufted, buttoned, corded, and draped. Curtains were heavy and elaborate. Everything was decorated—with inlay, paint, gilt, fringe, feathers, artificial flowers, mother-of-pearl. The effect was usually overdone and confused, with little unity. Historically, Victorian building has little significance, but some of it was both interesting and ingenious. The period saw the beginning of industrialism and mass production.

IN AMERICA

In the colonies, on this side of the ocean, there was no consistent style. The early settlers came from many European countries and settled in a variety of climates, from those of northern New England to the deep

2–12   A Regency table with book carrier.

South. There were roughly three periods: the early colonial (1620–1725), the one influenced by Georgian design (1725–1780), and the Federal, which followed the American Revolution. In general, the styles followed the English periods, but were adapted in personal and local ways. During the Federal period, for about fifty years after the colonies had become a nation, the style that developed was based on certain native qualities combined with French Empire and English Regency characteristics. Two outstanding architects were Charles Bulfinch and Samuel McIntire, both in New England. The best-known furniture designer was Duncan Phyfe. Elegant fabrics, damasks, brocades, and satins were popular. Subtle olive-greens, grays, and soft blues were used, or the bright colors of the flag.

The first expression of ideas that were later accepted by the architects who pioneered what has been termed the modern movement was by an American sculptor, Horatio Greenough (1805–1852). While most designers were basing their architecture on historical design, he warned (in a series of articles in the 1840's) against copying the past. He felt that if design were to move forward it must be organic and that forms must be adapted to their functions. He pointed out that the use of forms—even beautiful ones—for functions for which they were never intended, had led invariably from "perfection . . . to . . . decay." [2] Referring to the Greek masters, he advised: "We believe firmly that they can teach us; but let us learn principles, not copy shapes." [3]

2. Horatio Greenough, *Form and Function*, Harold A. Small, ed. (Berkeley, Calif.: University of California Press, 1962), p. 54.
3. *Ibid*, p. 65.

THE INDUSTRIAL REVOLUTION

In England, John Ruskin (1819–1900) pointed out the importance of art to everyday living. He protested the superficiality and decadence of the social foundations of art. This idea was accepted by the artists, who, convinced that no object was unworthy of their attention, became interested in crafts. One of these artists, William Morris (1839–1896), who had been trained as an architect, led the revolt against the superficial and confused esthetics of Victorian environment. Morris established a studio where handcrafted furnishings were made according to his specifications, and he is held to have laid the foundation for the modern movement in design by his opposition to the separation of art from daily life and his insistence that art was unimportant unless shared by all. His efforts to bring art to the people were manifest in his designs, which were simple and direct, with an emphasis on basic forms, handcrafted from sturdy materials.

On the whole, Victorian architects had little interest either in Morris' ideas or the Industrial Revolution and the new materials that it had made available. It was the engineers who were interested and who were contributing the most to contemporary environment. By their use of iron and iron combined with glass, they created a new kind of building, which, with its emphasis on structural function, was the forerunner of modern architecture. The most dramatic example of this kind of building was the Crystal Palace. Planned by a designer of greenhouses, Joseph Patton, it was built in London in 1851, and was exactly 1851 feet long. Com-

pleted in six months, it was constructed of glass panels and prefabricated cast-iron sections bolted together.

In France in 1863, the architect Viollet-le-Duc, lecturing at the École des Beaux-Arts in Paris, was enthusiastically applauded by students when he announced that all architecture of the future must be an expression of "steam, electricity, and speed." His advanced ideas were in accord with the new machine civilization and the use of new materials, such as steel. He saw new buildings not as works of art with beautiful façades, but as organic wholes, in which every part of the architecture was also part of a structural need.

ART NOUVEAU

Another style started in the 1890's with a house in Brussels designed by Victor Horta and spread over most of western Europe. Called Art Nouveau, it was a protest against the extreme eclecticism and the imitativeness of traditional design. Based on the idea that the forms of nature were a more valid source of inspiration than any classical forms, it made use of new materials, especially iron, and its organic, structural curves were covered with naturalistic decoration that was flowing, linear, and asymmetrical (Fig. 2–13). As a style it lasted less than three decades, partly because it had little relation to architecture. It

2–14 Dining room (Masters' Houses) by Moholy-Nagy, one of the early exponents of the Bauhaus.

that were not based on tradition, and their young apprentice, Frank Lloyd Wright, was expounding revolutionary ideas based on "organic" design. In Germany architects were making the most emphatic break with the past and had accepted the machine and the new materials and processes. The modern movement, which had been evolving since William Morris, culminated in the foundation of the Bauhaus in Germany in 1919, under the guidance of Walter Gropius. Its purpose was to unite art and life by creating forms typical of the machine age and to develop a genuinely contemporary architecture (Fig. 2–14). The consumer products designed at the Bauhaus were reproduced all over the world, and—of greater importance —it became a center of creative energy in Europe. The Bauhaus movement became international in its influence, and well-known artists and architects—former teachers at the Bauhaus—brought its ideas to the United States.

served the purpose of clearing away the clutter of excessive eclecticism, opening the way for a genuinely contemporary expression. Its influence remains, providing inspiration for many designers today.

"MODERN"

At about the same time, changes were taking place elsewhere. In Chicago Louis Sullivan and his partner, Dankmar Adler, were creating designs

Sullivan and Wright

Louis Sullivan (1856–1924), an original thinker, somewhat of a revolutionary and an innovator, worked in Chicago during the last quarter of the nineteenth century. He was disgusted with the weak eclecticism in

2–15 Typical transformation of a conventional "box" room into spaces, according to concepts formulated by Frank Lloyd Wright.

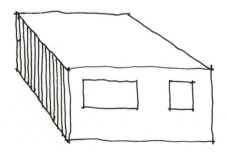 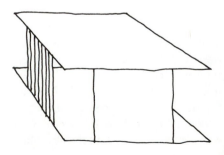

vogue and was determined to create a different kind of architecture that made use of the new engineering advances. Sullivan may be best known for his statement that "form follows function," but he added that "the function *created* or organized its form." He was the first architect to treat structure as logically integral to design, and the skeletons of his buildings are seen as the basis of their final form. While most architects were fighting the necessity for tallness in office buildings, Sullivan designed the first skyscraper, the Wainwright Building in St. Louis.

Frank Lloyd Wright (1869–1959) was a stormy, dramatic figure and an emphatically original thinker. To Wright a façade seemed structurally dishonest when it became a design in itself (as in Renaissance practice), with little relation to the interior. His buildings were organic, and began with their heart or core: "construction proceeding from the nature of a planned or organized inside to a consistent outside." [4] Thus, the exterior was the result of the need of the interior, and the whole an integrated structure, developed in the same manner as an organism. Space was not to be confined in boxlike rooms (Fig. 2–15). "The space to be lived in is now the human reality of the building and in terms of space we find the forms we seek." [5]

Wright's influence on environment was great. He was interested in every kind of structure and is famous for a skyscraper, churches and synagogues, office buildings, houses, and a monumental museum. He pioneered use of the cantilever in house construction and was particularly interested in materials, each to be used according to its own nature. He was an early champion of the machine, but used only as a tool, never as master. He loved the land and insisted that his houses have a kinship with the ground. He designed many different kinds of houses, each uniquely suited to its site, subtly fused with its surroundings to create a smooth, uninterrupted transition from natural to man-made environment (Fig. 2–16). His primary interest was in the house as a shelter, and he was concerned with the spirit as well as the quality of space. He created flexible, open floor plans, unlike those commonly in use at the time with their separate rooms connected by doors and hallways. In his houses environment was still enclosure and shelter, but with a feeling of freedom.

4. Frank Lloyd Wright, *Genius and the Mobocracy* (New York: Horizon Press, 1970), p. xiii.

5. *Ibid.*

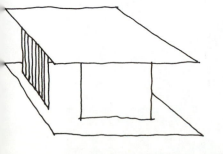
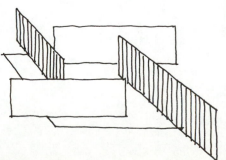
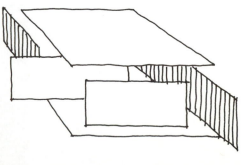

2–16 Wright's Taliesin East
interior (*above*) and exterior
(*below*). Note relatedness of
structure and site.

Gropius and Mies van der Rohe

Walter Gropius (1883–1969) was responsible for pulling together the many and varied elements that constituted the Bauhaus. "The strong desire to include every vital component of life instead of excluding part of them . . . has characterized my life," [6] he said. He brought together artists, craftsmen, architects, and product designers, including such men as Joseph Albers, Marcel Breuer, Paul Klee, Laszlo Moholy-Nagy, and later Mies van der Rohe, as teachers at the Bauhaus. Although Gropius is best known for this educational concept, his architecture was also significant. The buildings he designed for the school at Dessau have been called by critics the first real masterpiece of the modern movement. He came to the United States in 1937 as Chairman of Harvard's School of Architecture, where he introduced his theories and teaching methods and was active for almost thirty years.

Mies van der Rohe (1896–1969), one of the foremost disciples of the above-mentioned Bauhaus school, considered that technology, when it is of a high order, becomes architecture. The influences of Mies on environment have been very strong. Particularly influential are his skyscrapers and high-rise apartment houses, which are distinguished by their use of glass and steel in simple, straight lines, with reflecting surfaces, and notable for their clarity and sophistication. Best-known in this country is probably his Seagram Building in New York City, designed with Philip Johnson.

6. Walter Gropius, *Scope of Total Architecture* (New York: Harper & Row, 1955), p. xviii.

2–17   Mies van der Rohe's German Pavilion.

One of his earliest and most celebrated buildings, the German Pavilion in Barcelona (Fig. 2–17) (built in 1929, but unfortunately demolished in 1930) used space almost as a fluid. In the pavilion interior vertical planes defined the enclosed spaces without separating them, so that space was a continual experience, flowing from one area to another and from interior to exterior. Constructed of marble and travertine, glass walls, and steel supports, the building contained almost nothing, but the pure surfaces and elegant materials gave it the appearance of a jewel. In 1928 Mies designed for this pavilion a chair (Fig. 11–5) of stainless steel and leather that has become a modern classic.

Saarinen

Eero Saarinen (1910–1961), youngest of these contemporary architects, felt strongly that there was a danger that their design concepts would become automatic, applied as a formula over and over again. His philosophy of architecture includes six principles, all significant to environment: (1) respect for function; (2) structural integrity (when it contributes to the whole and advances the other principles); (3) awareness of our time; (4) emotional expression of the purpose and meaning of the building; (5) integration with environment; and (6) unity of design ("inside or outside, the building sings with the same message").

Saarinen's buildings are symbolic in the sense that the mood or spirit of the building is related to the function, which could not readily be mis-understood in any of his buildings; an industrial complex, for instance, could not be mistaken for a school or a school for a chapel. Saarinen used space sculpturally (Fig. 2–18) and his buildings are organic in the same sense that Wright's are. More than any other architect since Robert Adam, his interiors and exteriors are integrated, and everything inside, even furnishings if possible, is consistent in character and is part of the architecture. The Columbia Broadcasting System Building in New York City is a unique skyscraper, of reinforced concrete clad in dark granite. Its rugged profiles produce an exciting play of light and shadow.

2–18 Flight Center of Saarinen's TWA Building at Kennedy International Airport. Note consistency of architecture and furnishings.

Le Corbusier

Charles Edouard Jeanneret-Gris (1887–1965), called Le Corbusier, worked mainly in France. In his designs he used a modular system (called "Modulor"), based on the dimensions of the human body—that is, all the main dimensions of his buildings' living space are the same as or simple multiples of the average dimensions of the human body. He felt that this modular formula was so nearly perfect that its use made bad design difficult. Le Corbusier summed up human activities as living, working, circulating, and cultivating the mind and body, and postulated that any structural system in which these activities could be carried on must have unique qualities. He called a home "a machine for living," meaning that it should be planned with the same precision as a machine and should have comparable utility. His residences, typified by his

Villa Savoie (Fig. 2–19) outside of Paris, tend to be based on a skeleton supported by free-standing pillars. In this type of construction, load-bearing walls are unnecessary, and are replaced by what are essentially only screens, partly glass. The openness of the Villa Savoie's interior, unlike Wright's space (Fig. 2–16), grows out of a juxtaposition of many-sided shapes that seems to reflect his interest in cubism in painting. Also unlike Wright's approach is the separation of the house from the landscape. The flat, concrete roof, used for a roof garden, provides additional space. In others of his buildings, sunbreaks, used to keep the interior cool, give the façades a characteristic pattern of light and shade.

Le Corbusier favored built-in furniture and purely functional pieces that replaced furniture as such with equipment for the functions of living—eating, sleeping, sitting, bathing, and cleaning.

2–19 *At top,* Le Corbusier's Villa Savoie, near Paris. *Directly above,* part of the interior and terrace. Note contrast between structure and site.

2–20 *Above,* Le Corbusier's Notre-Dame-du-Haut, Ronchamps, France; *opposite,* an interior view.

The chapel of Notre-Dame-du-Haut (Fig. 2–20) at Ronchamps in France, probably the best known and most admired of Le Corbusier's buildings, provides a unique environment for worship. The walls inside and out are sweeping curves of whitewashed concrete. Shafts of light come from many rectangular windows of different sizes and shapes and from space between the walls and the roof. The roof, with a curve that reverses on the exterior and interior, appears to float in the air. The building is itself sculpture. Though some have criticized it, few are unaffected by it.

Kahn

Louis I. Kahn (1901–), generally considered one of the greatest living architects, has a deep concern for environment and the design of it. Unlike Wright, Gropius, Mies, and Le Corbusier, who started early, Kahn has taken twenty-five years to evolve his theory of architecture; it is, however, one that most architects feel to be thoroughly creative and comprehensive. He explains some basic principles:

Form encompasses a harmony of systems, a sense of Order and that which

characterizes one existence from another. Form has no shape or dimension. For example, in the differentiation of a spoon from spoon, spoon characterizes a form having two inseparable parts, the handle and the bowl. A spoon implies a specific design made of silver or wood, big or little, shallow or deep. Form is "what." Design is "how." Form is impersonal. Design belongs to the designer. Design is form-making in order.[7]

Kahn believes that buildings have "existence will," that the functions of space generate their own form, so

7. Vincent Scully, Jr., *Louis I. Kahn* (New York: George Braziller, 1962), p. 113.

that the architect must first understand the function in order to express it appropriately. There are two kinds of spaces—"served" (major spaces, such as rooms that are lived in) and "servant" (minor spaces, such as closets and equipment and maintenance areas).

In the Richards Medical Research Laboratories (Fig. 2–21) at the University of Pennsylvania in Philadelphia, Kahn, instead of placing the laboratories along a corridor, has stacked them in three towers that are located around an enclosed service tower. Rising dramatically above these are

2–21 Kahn's Richards Medical Research Laboratories, University of Pennsylvania, Philadelphia.

brick towers that house exhaust stacks and exit stairways. These supply "what the building wants"—vertical circulation and air. The contrast between the glass and the brick towers clearly differentiates between the "served" and the "servant" spaces. A recent major project of his in this country is the Jonas Salk Institute in San Diego, California.

Tange

A strong Japanese influence on American design is epitomized in the work of, among others, Kenzo Tange (1913–), who studied in Europe and became familiar with Western architecture before the Second World War. Tange has become a strong link between the architectural design of the Orient and of the Western world.

His work has much in common with Saarinen's, particularly its large-scale sculptural quality. With his intimate knowledge of Japanese tradition and his thorough understanding of international style, he has coordinated and harmonized—in method and style— the functional aspects of Western technology and traditional stylistic elements of many kinds in a variety of structures. His work, which can be found in countries around the world, has made him a very strong force in contemporary architecture.

DIVERSE DIRECTIONS

In the work of these pioneer architects there are qualities that are great. The Bauhaus had aimed to create a system of teaching art and craft that could meet all the demands of the new technology. In its emphasis on basic design, its purism, and its gospel of functionalism, it lost its feeling for the individual, became arbitrary and autocratic. But it had accomplished a great deal in breaking the dependencies on the past and had established systems of teaching in the field of art and design that are important and useful. Frank Lloyd Wright, at the other extreme, was a romantic individualist and, like Le Corbusier, intended that his design would reaffirm the importance of the human being. But their work was also arbitrary and autocratic.

Although each of these architects of the modern movement is strongly individualistic, the work of the early ones had developed, for the most part, in the same general direction until the First World War. They had certain theories in common; they agreed that design for environment began with space and must be organic. Although not all the forms they developed were alike, they were unlike the forms of earlier architecture. They used new constructional methods and materials. They made full use of the machine in their design concepts, synthesizing the aims of their architecture in a new way. However, as each developed, extending and refining his ideas, he went in his own direction; with the increase in the palette of modern materials and construction methods, this was logical. The two extremes of this diversity of directions are represented by Mies and Le Corbusier. Mies' approach is exemplified by his Farnsworth House (Fig. 2–22), built in

2–22 Mies van der Rohe's Farnsworth House exterior (*above*), and interior (*below*).

Plano, Illinois. It is a rectangle with a travertine floor, walled partly by sheets of plate glass and partly with metal screening. Except for a central core which holds the fireplace, bathroom, and utilities, the space is totally unified. This concept starts with technologically motivated form, with human use adjusted to that form. Le Corbusier, on the other hand, became more interested in the plastic potentials of architecture, which he achieved through his imaginative use of concrete, as in his chapel at Ronchamps. Employing an approach opposite to that of Mies, his concept is based primarily on the emotional, physical, and intellectual needs of the human being (his "modular man"), around which all structural or technical aspects are planned.

This constrast illustrates the direction in which the architecture begun in the twenties has gone. Out of the Mies theories, a technically motivated neoclassicism has developed that follows his concepts and often his forms. One of the most influential exponents of this style—in his architecture as well as in his writing—is Philip Johnson. The sculpturally active, plastic direction taken by Le Corbusier and by Wright in his later work (sometimes called brutalism) has many followers, of whom Paul Rudolph is a good example. Louis Kahn, partly because of his theories and mainly because of the dates of his late-flowering achievement, seems to constitute an influence transitional between such men as Johnson and Rudolph, the followers of the pioneers, who are now doing their finest work.

Today more kinds of materials are available, and there are more ways to build that are practical, functional, and economical. Such potential has never before existed. Almost no new buildings based on traditional design are being built today, for it is impossible, both economically and vocationally, to duplicate the craftsmanship that made the old buildings so beautiful.

Architecture today is marked by what might be termed antistyle. There is plenty of style, both good and bad, but not a single *style* characteristic of the time. Each individual can express himself and his ideas in his work, and there are few limits.

In *World Architecture* 2, John Donat says:

There seems to be a real danger that the technocrats roaring into the field of industrialized buildings are devising a plurality of brilliant techniques to construct environment that no one wants to live in . . . . the real issues are philosophical, not technological, not *how* to build, but *what* to build.[8]

Yet the Italian engineer Pier Luigi Nervi feels that technology and esthetics not only go hand in hand, but complement each other. "The new materials, in particular reinforced concrete and steel, have form-giving possibilities, derived from their technological characteristics, that are completely different from the wood or masonry materials of the past." [9] He is convinced that "there is a full and intrinsic agreement between aesthetic expression and the static and construction requirements." This, as he sees it, will result in "good aesthetic expression."

8. John Donat, ed., *World Architecture* 2 (New York: Viking Press, 1965), p. 8.
9. Pier Luigi Nervi, quoted in Gyorgy Kepes, "Function Follows His Forms," *New York Times Book Review*, January 30, 1966, p. 3.

BIBLIOGRAPHY

ALLSOPP, BRUCE; BOOTON, HAROLD W.; AND CLARK, URSULA. *The Great Tradition of Western Architecture* (Architectural Book Publishing, 1966). The growth of the Western tradition in architecture from ancient Greece to the present. Brief text with many excellent illustrations and some drawings.

BANHAM, REYNER. *Guide to Modern Architecture* (Architectural Press, 1962). Function, form, construction, and space in modern architecture. Illustrations with commentary. An emphatic and well-informed point of view.

BERNIER, G., AND R., eds. *The Best in 20th Century Architecture* (Reynal, 1964). Modern architecture to 1964, from an international viewpoint. Includes material on some lesser-known forerunners of modern architecture. Readable text and fine illustrations; from European art review *L'Oeil*.

DONAT, JOHN, ed. *World Architecture 2* (Viking Press, 1965). Building projects, ideas, and excellent comment from seventeen countries. Also Nos. 1, 3, and 4.

FITCH, JAMES MARSTON. *Architecture and the Esthetics of Plenty* (Columbia University Press, 1961). A critical evaluation of American architecture, emphasizing conflict between quantity and quality. Witty and easy to read.

HITCHCOCK, HENRY-RUSSELL. *Architecture: Nineteenth and Twentieth Centuries*, 2nd ed. (Penguin, 1963). Authoritative; easy to read.

HITCHCOCK, HENRY-RUSSELL, et al. *World Architecture: A Pictorial History* (McGraw-Hill, 1963). An elegant history of architecture with a fine introduction by Henry-Russell Hitchcock. Sections on ancient, classical, Chinese, Japanese, Indian, Islamic, Medieval, Renaissance, and modern (to the sixties) architecture by seven authorities.

HOFMANN, WERNER, AND KULTERMANN, UDO. *Modern Architecture* (Viking Press, 1969). A handsome presentation of solutions to design problems in buildings from the mid-nineteenth century to the present. One hundred and twelve photographs (color) with floor plans and commentary.

JONES, CRANSTON. *Architecture Today and Tomorrow* (McGraw-Hill, 1961). Biographical material on twenty-five architects, going back to Louis Sullivan. Informative and easy to read; well-chosen illustrations.

JORDAN, R. FURNEAUX. *A Concise History of Western Architecture* (Harcourt Brace Jovanovich, 1970). Easy to read; contemporary approach. Emphasizes close relationship between architecture and society.

KAUFMANN, EDGAR, ed. *The Rise of an American Architecture* (Praeger, 1970). A series of essays by architectural historians combine to give a clear, appreciative account of the development of a specifically American architecture. Excellent illustrations.

MANSBRIDGE, JOHN. *Graphic History of Architecture* (Viking Press, 1967). How social and economic conditions resulted in particular kinds of buildings, and the interaction between technique and style. Highly visual; many drawings, including perspectives, isometrics, cutaways, plans, and elevations. Also information on materials and how they were used.

MC COY, ESTHER. *Five California Architects* (Reinhold, 1960). Thoroughly readable description of the work of five California architects who combined adaptation with innovation in creating styles that were individual yet appropriate to the materials available and the particular environment. Foreword by John Entenza.

MUMFORD, LEWIS. *Roots of Contemporary Architecture* (Dover, 1966). Essays by twenty-nine writers, including Henry David Thoreau, Frank Lloyd Wright, and Sigfried Giedion. Fine source material.

———. *Sticks and Stones*, rev. ed. (Dover, 1955). Study of American architecture and civilization. Rewarding if one agrees with Mumford; interesting if not.

MUSCHENHEIM, WILLIAM. *Elements of the Art of Architecture* (Viking Press, 1964). Photographs illustrate the elements of architecture as manifested in building from the Greeks to the present. Similarities and contrasts are made clear by the juxtaposition of photographs. With explanatory captions and a brief résumé of major periods of Western architecture.

PARKER, ALFRED BROWNING. *You and Architecture* (Dial Press, 1965). Much information and excellent photographs.

PEHNT, WOLFGANG, ed. *Encyclopedia of Modern Architecture* (Abrams, 1964). Good reference material by thirty-one authorities from more than a dozen countries.

PETER, JOHN. *Masters of Modern Architecture* (George Braziller, 1958). Excellent introduction and brief résumé of architectural history. Each architect speaks for himself through selected writings. Fine illustrations.

PEVSNER, NIKOLAUS. *An Outline of European Architecture* (Penguin, 1960). The classic of European architectural history; an excellent reference. Some of Pevsner's ideas are being rethought by contemporary architects.

———. *Pioneers of Modern Design* (Penguin, 1969). Deals with period from William Morris to Walter Gropius.

RASMUSSEN, STEEN EILER. *Experiencing Architecture* (MIT Press, 1959). A happy, understandable approach to architecture; delightful reading.

ROOT, JOHN WILLIAM. *The Meanings of Architecture*, ed. by Donald Hoffmann (Horizon Press, 1967). Well organized, easy to read, and illuminating. Root's influence was considerable.

3

3–1 View of galleries in Wright's Guggenheim Museum, New York.

PRINCIPLES AND ELEMENTS

OF DESIGN

To design is to create an arrangement of parts that gives order and tangible expression to an idea. Louis I. Kahn has suggested that the idea is the skeleton and the process of development, design. In this process basic principles are applied in order to develop a system of "coordinated elements" suitable to the purpose or need. A design problem is any question posed or need defined that can be solved through this process of designing. The need can be for a particular vessel for pouring liquid or a structure for sitting or for an attractive and comfortable living room. Decorative design is different, and implies ornament added to an existing design or object.

DESIGN SOURCES

Design starts with an idea, the two basic sources of which are structures or patterns in nature and mathematics, insofar as one may think of mathematics as apart from nature. Over the centuries the results of ap-
plying both in solving problems of design and decoration have created a kind of secondary source, a vast reservoir of designs that have come themselves to serve as origins for new designs and to embody symbolism and tradition as handed down in manmade forms. Some ancient ideas have persisted virtually unchanged since their inception—the idea of the sunburst, for example. Others have evolved, changing over the centuries until the prototype is no longer recognizable. Probably the most basic design source in nature is an organism, with organs that differ in function but are mutually dependent. Any whole that is organized from parts that work together and are mutually dependent is "organic." A building or an object is organic when the parts grow out of a core idea—from the inside to a consistent outside—and are all integral parts of the whole. All Frank Lloyd Wright buildings are designed in this way; his Guggenheim Museum (Fig. 3–1), for example, bears a close resemblance to a spiral shell.

The natural environment surrounds us with infinitely varied design sources (Fig. 3–2). A leaf, a fern frond as it uncoils, a piece of coral, a shell, driftwood—all offer ideas for the designer. The skeleton of a fish, the human anatomy, the major physiological systems of animals and insects, provide fascinating specimens of structure. A honeycomb has as its basic unit a hexagonal structure that has been used in many kinds of design, both structural and decorative. The variety of flower, insect, bird, and plant forms is endless, and how many designs have been inspired by the egg shape? In addition to those that can be readily seen by the unaided eye, hosts of other sources have been added by the use of the microscope, telescope, and camera. Spirals whose parts show a logarithmic relationship are found in the shell of the chambered nautilus, the curve of an elephant's tusk, and the center of a daisy. This Fibonacci sequence—so called after its discoverer—is produced by starting with 1 and adding the last two numbers to arrive at the next: for example, 1, 1, 2, 3, 5, 8, 13, 21, 34. The parts of the daisy's spiral have the relationship 21:34, which is the same as that of the Golden Mean (see p. 50).

Many design principles are readily recognizable in nature: Symmetry is obvious in a leaf, a snowflake, various mineral crystals, and most insect and animal bodies. There is rhythm in a climbing vine, leaves on a branch, roads winding through hills. Texture is everywhere—in the gravel underfoot, in tree bark, the scales of a fish, or the smooth polished surface of wood. There are infinite examples of variety within unity, varying parts composed in a unified whole, par-

ticularly well illustrated by almost any tree. Living forms in nature are rarely static, but have a feeling of growth and movement.

The study of these forms and processes of nature and of their application to design deals with design fundamentals, and is sometimes called basic design. This approach, which grew out of Bauhaus ideas, is based on the endless variety of forms that results from the combination and recombination of the same elements in different ways. It is intended to be sufficiently flexible to be continuously open to change, as an organism is. In applying these natural forces to design, the method emphasizes the process rather than the result. Perception, with an awareness of materials, tools, and processes (and the ability to control them), is developed through exploration that is emotional as well as intellectual. Visual quality is an added result.

While many natural forms are geometric, geometry in itself is as important a source of design as nature, and its possibilities for design are infinite. Any design pattern that consists of a repeated motif or group of motifs has a geometric basis. Geometric forms are generally restrained, but not necessarily static, and are often used to provide a stable base when combined with free forms or irregular shapes, which are visually more active (Fig. 3–3).

In ancient times, according to Bruno Munari, the square "signified the idea of enclosure, of house, of settlement" and is "present in all styles of all people in all periods, both as a structural element and as a surface to support or determine a particular form of decoration. It is static if it stands on its side and dynamic if it

3–2 Some design sources in nature—a seashell, snowflake, honeycomb, and fish skeleton.

3–3 Interior of Moore's Gallery House, Washington, D.C., in which both geometric and irregular forms are employed.

stands at an angle."[1] Many forms can be derived from the square, and all other rectangles and the cube are, of course, simple variations on it. Even though the circle is a dynamic form, its curve is the simplest; with neither beginning nor end, it has, since ancient times, represented eternity. Munari points out that "People form a circle spontaneously when they want to observe something together. This probably gave rise to the arena, the circus, and the trading post in the stock exchange."[2] Regular figures of more than four sides make an endless variety of design elements, as do regularly curving forms such as ellipses, sections of a cone, which is itself a three-dimensional form with many applications.

Man-made objects, created in answer to some need, themselves often offer a source of design—telephone wires, for example, tools, a woodpile, and machinery of all kinds are infinite in their visual possibilities. Many

1. Bruno Munari, *The Discovery of the Square* (New York: George Wittenborn, 1962), p. 5.

2. Bruno Munari, *The Discovery of the Circle* (New York: George Wittenborn, 1965), p. 29.

structures originated for roofing over or bridging spaces—such as the post and lintel, the arch, and the vault and dome—have similar design potential.

One of the more progressive and original designers of modern environment, R. Buckminster Fuller, considers the universe his basic design source: "I did not set out to design a house that hung from a pole [Dymaxion House] or to develop a geodesic dome... I started with the universe as an organization of regenerative principles.... My objective was humanity's success in the universe." From one of these "regenerative" principles, Fuller isolated a mathematical sequence of development that was the basis of his "geodesic dome" (Fig. 3-4), which is capable of enclosing maximum space with minimum stress and great economy. Later he found a similar structure in nature—in the bone structure of certain marine organisms whose surfaces are subject to great stress. Thus, Fuller arrived at an existing natural principle through the development of a mathematical one; most design has more than one possible origin.

A design has often reflected some functional or emotional need, as well as regional influences—such as climate and the availability, locally, of certain materials. In colonial New Mexico, for example, the need for shelter was answered with buildings of bricks made from local earth and straw, held together with mortar made from the same mud. The houses and churches that resulted seem to grow from the ground. Roofs were flat, walls thick, and windows small to keep out the heat of the sun. In contrast, in New England, where severe winters required roofs that could shed snow, steeply pitched roofs were more com-

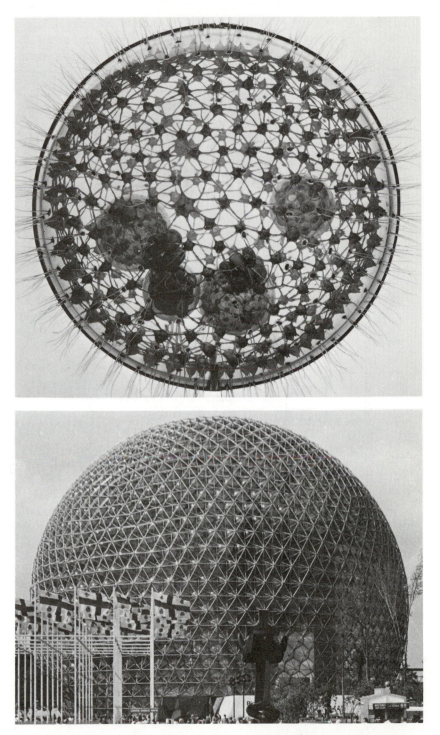

3-4 *Above*, a marine protozoan that exhibits the structural basis of Buckminster Fuller's "geodesic dome," *below*.

mon. Towers and steeples became decorative, but they began as an answer to the need for guarding a village or for communicating by means of lanterns or bells.

DESIGN PRINCIPLES

There can be no interior without space. There may never be complete agreement about the conception of space, but it is the first requisite for any interior. Actual space, in terms of interior design, can be defined as the area to be organized within enclosing forms. Visual space is apparent or sensed space and may include reflections in mirrors and areas beyond any transparent enclosures. The architect usually determines the forms that solve the spatial and functional problems and the interior designer plans the best way to develop and enhance this spatial solution. For best results the architect and the interior designer work together from the beginning of the planning process. The design for the space should be based on an underlying concept, a central idea developed into a scheme according to which color and all the other elements are combined with the necessary furnishings to create an integrated whole.

UNITY

Unity, oneness, a totality of related parts, is absolutely essential to successful design. The principle of unity encompasses all the other principles of design. It is achieved by choosing and arranging parts, both space and objects, that produce an orderly and esthetically pleasing whole. Leonardo da Vinci's observation is a practical one: "Every part is disposed to unite with the whole that it may thereby escape its own incompleteness." And Eero Saarinen has said that wherever you are in a building that has this quality of unity, it "sings with the same message." The whole, in such a building, is more than the sum of its parts. In a correctly designed interior every part of the space and every object in it contributes to the total effect, *each depending on the others*, and in doing so, each appears at its best. Such an interior will have consistent sizes and shapes, a sense of order, and a feeling of repose. Its scheme is built around a central idea to which all incidental design gives support. Colors, walls, floor and ceiling treatment, and furnishings and decorative objects—all will have some quality of purpose and appearance in common; in a unified interior, the eye is not tempted to jump from one thing to another (Fig. 3–5).

Aids to achieving unity are an orderly and logical plan that is thoroughly understood; a center of interest that determines the character of the space; and sufficient emphasis on that center so that its role as a center is unmistakable. Repetition and similarity contribute to unity, but too much of either may result in a monotonous and uninteresting design.

[In evaluating the unity of an interior, these questions can be asked: (1) Is the treatment consistent with the basic idea? (If it is elegant in character, for example, do the materials and arrangement support this feeling?) (2) Are too many materials or colors used? (3) Does all the design, in properly varying degrees of strength, give support to the basic idea? (4) Is there sufficient variety to assure an interesting composition without interfering with the harmony?]

LINE

In the design of interior space for environment, line is so taken for granted that its effect is sometimes overlooked. A line can be simply a thin mark, the trace of a moving point, the edge that defines a flat form, or the outline of a solid object. A line is versatile and can define or limit shape, divide areas, suggest movement, speed, or direction. It provides the basis for all pattern and two-dimensional decoration, and can be bold or weak, rhythmic or static, clumsy or delicate, rigid or fluid. Some convey excitement, restlessness, nervousness, or activity; others, an impression of monotony or strength. They should be used subtly; if the occupant of a room is conscious of lines as such, there are probably too many.

⌈In an interior, straight lines—vertical, horizontal, or diagonal—give a feeling of strength and severity. Vertical lines tend to be strongest and have a structural feeling, suggesting the vertical supports used in building. Vertical lines, whether in doorways, windows or other architectural features, or in wallpaper or furnishings, help to suggest height in a room.⌉

⌈Horizontal lines are less strong than vertical lines, and are fundamentally more restful. (It has been suggested that human reaction to lines is based on the fact that when man is in action he is vertical and when resting, horizontal.) Horizontal lines can relieve or diminish the effects of strong vertical ones. In a room they can be provided by tables, benches, desks, chairs or sofas, by the tops of doorways, windows, fireplaces. Too many horizontals may make a room calm to the point of dullness.⌉

⌈Diagonal lines are more difficult to use successfully. They seem to be pointing into space, and unless decisively stopped, are likely to keep the eye moving right out of the room. Diagonal lines are lines of action, and when not properly controlled, can be annoying. The herringbone pattern tends to avoid this, since in it, lines meet to form V's, giving a sense of completion and neutralizing the restlessness of simple diagonals. Diagonal lines that are too dominant in a room —in the arrangement of one wall, for instance—can disrupt the room's basic⌉

3–5 An interior that combines a variety of furnishings in a unified way.

3–6 Straight and curved lines combined to produce an airy effect in the Oval Salon, Hôtel de Soubise, Paris.

structural form and destroy its unity. All curved lines—mathematical and especially freehand—are livelier and more fun than straight ones, and generally seem more graceful, soft, and subtle. A mathematical curve is made with an instrument, using as a basis any part of the arc of a circle or ellipse. The curve based on the former is less subtle than that using the arc of an ellipse, which is changing its direction at a varying rate at any point and thus allows for more variety. There is no end to the variety of skillfully drawn freehand curves. Differences in subtlety in such curves can be made evident by contrasting a Victorian chair leg or picture with a Louis XV chair leg or picture. While good freehand curves give a feeling of airiness, they lack strength, and if they are not to seem weak rather than airy their use in relation to straight lines must be planned carefully (Fig. 3–6).

Many curved lines in a room produce a restless effect. This can be corrected by strengthening the straight lines or, of course, eliminating some of the curved ones, or both. On the other hand, the stiffness of a room with many straight lines can be relieved by the introduction of curved lines.

Lines used in surface design or decoration—in wallpaper, fabrics, decorative ornament, and floor coverings—are important to the general design of a space. In any interior space, design lines, some of which are only suggested by the direction of some actual lines, are also a basic part of the design. Diagonal lines appear to move in a direction; angles tend to direct the eye toward their intersection, which points to something; strong curves tend to move in the direction of their greatest thrust (Fig. 3–10). Any feeling of motion in a line must be controlled so that it is a rhythmic part of the unity. Lines may also have a dynamic effect on each other (Fig. 3–7).

FORM

[Form is the arrangement of lines or planes so that they represent something, from a simple geometric shape, such as a triangle, to an object of utility, such as a desk or chair. Each view of any object may give a different impression of the lines or planes that form it. Form is less easily per-ceived than color because it requires a response more intellectual than emotional. Most forms can be traced to some geometric source or sources. A successful design for any interior space requires forms that are not only individually well designed, but that complement each other and are appropriate to the space and its function. A certain amount of diversity of forms is usually desirable, so long as the different forms are harmonious.

According to Steen Eiler Rasmussen, the Danish architect, people react to forms as hard or soft, regardless of the material used, on the basis of their early visual and tactile experiences. A form can also give an impression of heaviness or lightness, depending on the material (and particularly the texture — see below — of the material) from which it is made.]

3–7 Sofa at rug edge and desk tops at rear create a visual line in this office interior.

BALANCE

Balance is the relation of parts that creates a sense of repose and of completion in a room. Balance may be axial, with parts organized on either side of an actual or implied axis, or radial, with parts organized around an actual or implied central point. Both kinds can be symmetrical or asymmetrical (Figs. 3–8 and 3–9). When the elements on either side of an axis or around a focal point are identical, or approximately so, the balance is symmetrical. Asymmetrical balance results when unlike forces—objects of different size, shape, and/or color— are used together in such a way as to create a feeling of equilibrium. Lack of balance in a room can make an occupant uncomfortable, although he may not know why.

Symmetrical balance is simple and may be obvious. It gives a feeling of stability and permanence and can be used in the treatment of a whole space or room or of one part of it, as a wall or a furniture grouping. It is more likely to reflect order and intelligence than spontaneity and imagination, and used in a plodding, literal way, it can be static and inflexible. Because it conveys dignity, it is often used in formal rooms. Sometimes it lacks warmth and vigor, but it can be inventive and original, and many of

3–8　Axial, symmetrical balance in a living room.

the finest rooms designed and built in France, Italy, and England in the seventeenth and eighteenth centuries were symmetrical in design.

Where casualness is desired, asymmetrical design is usually more effective. Being less formal, it permits more personal expression and variety, and can create more exciting and dramatic effects. With it, one large object can be balanced by a group of smaller ones, or a small, bright or dark object by a larger, soft- or light-colored one. Texture, pattern, and lighting are useful in helping to achieve successful asymmetry in a space. Asymmetrical balance allows for more freedom but demands more

skill in its handling; it can be beautifully subtle when successful.

SCALE AND PROPORTION

Scale refers to the size of objects—chairs, rooms, buildings—in relation to each other and to the human body, the basis for all scale. It is because of differences in scale that a human being seems large in a small room and small in a large room—tiny, for example, in the great spaces of the Pantheon. Good scale is the result of a pleasing relationship among the components of a space or room and between them and the whole. Thus, all furnishings should be scaled to

3–9 Asymmetrical balance.

people, to each other, and to the space in which they are used.

Proportion, closely related to scale, is the relationship of masses and areas of things (Fig. 3–10). The apparent dimensions involved can be affected by elements in the space other than actual dimensions—for example, color, value, texture, pattern, and light. Good proportion requires relationships that we sense as harmonious. A chair is well proportioned if its height, width, depth, and thickness of seat and various parts make a pleasing whole.

The Golden Mean or the Golden Section of the Greeks, consistently used as a rule for good proportion, postulates that two lines or areas are visually most effective together if the smaller is to the larger as the larger is to the whole. Le Corbusier's "Modulor" concept sought to link this proportion with the average size of the human body and of its principal elements—the leg, the forearm, and

3–10 Good proportion in a Victorian apartment with modern furnishings.

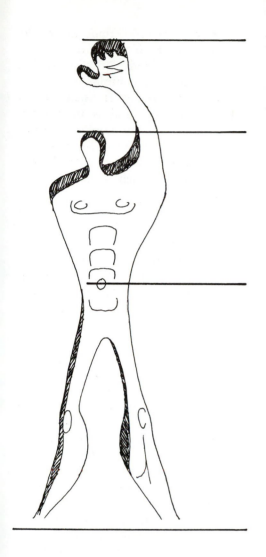

7'-5"

6'-0"

3'-8½"

A   G   B

C   D

F   D

E

3–11   How Le Corbusier's Modulor concept relates major elements of the human body to the proportions of the Golden Mean.

so on—as is shown in the illustration of the two concepts (Fig. 3–11).

RHYTHM

Rhythm is disciplined movement marked by a generally regular recurrence of elements, a measured repetition of accents (Fig. 3–12). It organizes and reflects the organization of spaces and forms in an interior in a way that helps the eye to recognize the order of the design. Rhythm may be subdued or dynamic, but it is al-

ways controlled. Uncontrolled movement can be distracting and make a room appear restless. Contrast and variety (see below) are important to rhythm.

Rhythm can be achieved in three ways. The commonest kind makes use of simple repetition or recurrence of form, pattern, color, or value (see Chapter 5, *Color*). Colors that are close in hue and value have little effect, while strongly contrasting ones may be as important to a rhythm as the pattern. Rhythm by simple repe-

3–12 Rhythm by repetition and progression demonstrated in the forms of the chapel of the Boston Government Center.

furniture, picture arrangement, the headboard of a bed, and so on.

The third kind of rhythm is that produced by a continuous but regularly varying line. It usually has a flowing quality, and is most often used in borders and framing elements, as cornices, windows, curtains, and rugs 'and is also frequent in all-over repeat designs, such as those in many fabrics and wallpapers.

Frequently, more than one kind of rhythm is used in a design: a continuous rhythm often has recurring motifs; progression of size or shape may also be repeated in a border or an all-over pattern. All three kinds of rhythm can be used successfully together.

EMPHASIS

Emphasis involves visual dominance and subordination, in which greater importance is given certain parts of a design while the others become secondary. In a good design a viewer will sense the relative importance of the various elements. If all—or even several important ones—are of equal importance, there is a feeling of competition and of a lack of coordination. If a center of interest is determined early in a plan and sufficiently emphasized, all parts of the design can then be given their suitable degree of dominance or subordination in the composition as a whole. Dominance and subordination can be achieved through use of color or value contrasts, directional lines, dimension, shape (a square in the midst of circles, for example), arrangement of objects, or concentration of detail. (With respect to the latter, too much pattern in any one area dilutes the emphasis and can destroy the spatial composition of the room, making the detail

tition is easy to use, but can lack subtlety and may become monotonous.

Progressive rhythm, a gradual change in the size, direction, and/or color of forms in a design, can be effective and dramatic. This kind of rhythm permits the use of more originality, and is usually stronger, more dynamic, and carries the eye more daringly than rhythm by repetition. It is more difficult to use successfully and improperly used may look like a stepladder. Colors can change in hue as well as value—moving, for example, through a series of hues that are consecutive in the spectrum, as in the sequence blue, blue-green, green. Progressive rhythm, then, can be seen in many and diverse manifestations—

more readily seen than the surface or form it is on.)

CONTRAST

Contrast, important to emphasis, is achieved by relating distinctly opposing elements or qualities—of line, form, texture, color, or value—especially in adjacent areas: the closer the opposed elements, the greater the contrast (Fig. 3–13). Too great contrast can produce an unfavorable reaction and destroy the unity of a space.

VARIETY

Variety can invest a design with individuality or surprise (Fig. 3–14); it can make the difference between a room that is pleasant and an exciting, or special one. Of course, the vitality it can provide, if not used with restraint, can destroy unity.

TEXTURE

Texture, the character of surface that is known primarily through touch, also has a visual quality (Fig. 3–15). The light and shadow of a rough-cut piece of granite and the cool, shiny surface of a piece of polished marble have both tactile and visual effects. Texture can be visually light or heavy, warm or cool, dense, open, regular, or irregular. In fabrics it can give a crisp, tailored look, or a soft and graceful one.

Texture affects the appearance of color. Two materials of different textures, tweed and satin, for example, dyed an identical color, will seem of different colors. The rough tweed absorbs the light, and its unevenness creates shadows that make it appear darker than the smooth, reflective satin. (It is important to look at any texture in a light as close as possible

3–13 Strong contrasts of form, texture, and color in an apartment interior.

3–14 Variety invests an otherwise straightforward interior with a special interest.

3–15 Harmonizing and contrasting textures in an interior.

to the kind in which it will be seen in the finished design.)

Contrasting textures offer an extra ingredient in the design of an interior and can readily enhance the appearance of a single object or piece of furniture. It is possible to gain diversity, variety, and drama in an interior of one hue through the use of contrasting textures.

PATTERN

Pattern is a usually orderly arrangement of two- or three-dimensional ornaments. Motifs may be natural, conventionalized, or abstract: those that copy the forms of nature fairly accurately are called natural or realistic; those taken from nature but adapted or simplified to fit a design are called conventionalized; and abstract motifs may be free forms or combinations of geometric ones.

Pattern—whether small, all-over repeats or large-scale, complicated motifs, and whether used traditionally or abstractly—has movement and should be used so that it flows with the rhythm of the design and never against it (Fig. 3–16). Properly used pattern is scaled to the design of the space, and its strength or quantity should not compete with the center of interest of the space.

UNIQUENESS

The interior designer needs to understand all the above-mentioned principles and elements if he is to achieve a satisfactory solution of a problem. When he becomes sufficiently familiar with them, he is ready to supply an added ingredient to the design— "uniqueness," which, Roger Fry has said, is as important to good design as is the order that is based on principles or law. Uniqueness in a design fulfills a human need for variety, chance, and the unforeseeable.

BIBLIOGRAPHY

ANDERSON, DONALD M. *The Elements of Design* (Holt, Rinehart and Winston, 1961). Decorative design and ornament in relation to design as a whole. Excellent and varied illustrations.

BALLINGER, LOUISE, AND VROMAN, T. *Design Sources and Resources* (Reinhold, 1965). Elementary and interesting text on the origins of design. Fine illustrations.

BATES, KENNETH F. *Basic Design* (World, 1960). An introduction to design principles called (correctly) by the author a "why-to-do-it" book. Encourages imaginative experimenting.

BEVLIN, M. E. *Design Through Discovery* (Holt, Rinehart and Winston, 1963). Excellent material on design origins.

BLOSSFELDT, KARL. *Art Forms in Nature* (Zwemmer, 1932). Introduction by Karl Nierendorf; no text. One hundred and twenty beautiful photographs of "examples from the Plant World. Direct from Nature."

CRANE, WALTER. *The Bases of Design* (Bell and Sons, 1909). A unique approach to the bases of the arts of design—architecture, utility, material and method, climate, race, symbolism, naturalism. The author was prominent in the design world of the late nineteenth century.

HUMBERT, CLAUDE. *Ornamental Design* (Viking, 1970). One thousand illustrations of ornamental forms. Gives origin and practical application in textiles, clay, wood, metal, and synthetics. Text is in French, English, and German.

ITTEN, JOHANNES. *Design and Form* (Reinhold, 1966). Author (who organized the basic course at the Bauhaus) gives a clear picture of the methods and aims of the early Bauhaus. One hundred and ninety-seven illustrations.

KEPES, GYORGY, ed. *The Man-Made Objects* (George Braziller, 1966). Fifteen prominent thinkers (among others, Marcel Breuer, Françoise Choay, Christopher Alexander, and Marshall McLuhan) discuss aspects of designing. Many fine illustrations.

NELSON, GEORGE. *Problems of Design* (Whitney, 1957). Problems of design, art, architecture, houses, planning, and interiors clearly and astutely analyzed. Treatises on Le Corbusier's Villa Savoie and Fuller's geodesic dome are excellent.

PEVSNER, NIKOLAUS. *The Sources of Modern Architecture and Design* (Praeger, 1968). The best of Pevsner's books from a design standpoint. Excellent for reference. Includes biographical notes.

SULLIVAN, LOUIS. A *System of Architectural Ornament* (Eakins, 1967). Foreword by Ada Louise Huxtable. Sullivan's humanistic philosophy and his theory of ornamental design clearly illustrated through his drawings. An essential book for designers.

3–16 Patterns supplement the forms to which they are applied.

4

In modern interior design, the floor plan, furniture arrangement, floor, wall, and window treatment, and decoration are coordinated with the architectural design. Results are best when the designer works with the architect in the various stages of the planning. Thus, as the contemporary designer of interior environment becomes increasingly concerned with space as well as surface and enclosures, his need for more technical information grows. It is possible, however, to understand the architectural approach without becoming an architect, and architectural schematic planning of space is combined, in this chapter, with the steps that follow to complete the design.

As the designer proceeds with the planning process, the design principles and elements discussed in Chapter 3 must be considered with each step. Any or all—line, form, balance, emphasis and contrast, variety, rhythm, scale and proportion—may be involved, and the result must have unity. Every part of the design must be examined carefully as it is developed, if the principles that do apply are to be used properly. The more consistently a theme is carried out— with principles unified and integrated —the more successful the design, regardless of the style or styles chosen.

PROGRAM

The planning process has essentially four steps: (1) formulation of the program requirements, which is a clear statement of the problem or problems; (2) a schematic, graphic representation of the requirements without regard for dimensions, but indicating proposed space relationships and traffic from space to space considered both functionally and esthetically; (3) the design development phase, in which sketches or models and necessary samples are used in working out all facets of the design, from the floor plan to (4) the final presentation.

The program requirements include a description of the space to be used, photographs of it (if an existing building), photographs of the view (if possible), elevations and floor plans, in-

THE PLANNING PROCESS

formation on usable exterior areas and on the activities and functions that each space must serve, and finally, the personal preferences of the client with respect to materials and furnishings.

Thus, typical of the questions a designer must answer at this stage are: What will the client be doing in the various spaces? How does he want to feel in each space and in moving from one to another? What does he wish to see or hear? What does he want others to see or hear? What relationship is wanted between adjoining spaces—privacy or ease of communication—and should they appear separate or connected, alike or contrasting?

How a building relates to the exterior background is a factor in determining the treatment of the interior. Also important to the designer is whether an interior space will open onto an exterior space that is to be used. In such cases the inside and outside spaces should also be properly related as to function and circulation, which make the kind of exposure and climate at the site important. Although advances in heating and cooling technology have made it possible to have an open house in a cold climate and closed buildings where it is hot, such things as direction of the sun in any room where there is exposure must be considered. For example, a dining room with floor-to-ceiling glass, facing west, would receive uncomfortably direct light at dinner time unless shading devices or overhangs were included. Choice of materials and types of construction must also be considered in relation to climate.

Throughout the programing phase, requirements should be evaluated in relation to the mood and character of the total scheme as it develops, so that terms and premises that may have been vague are clarified for both client and designer.

A request, for example, for a "luxurious" living room can mean, among other things, a desire for more space, a higher ceiling, elegant materials, or rare pieces of furniture. Other questions might arise in the same case: Will the budget cover the luxury wanted? Is the client aware of such design devices as overhang, or a wall extension beyond a floor-to-ceiling

57

glass wall, which add visual space without significantly increasing costs? Finally, it is important to keep in mind that it is impossible to complete any interior. Tastes and environmental needs change and things wear out, so that any normal interior will continue to grow and develop. To some extent this growth can be anticipated, and the possibilities for future expansion should be made a part of the original plan.

GRAPHIC PROGRAM SOLUTION

When the program requirements are completed, the designer submits a graphic program solution, with preliminary budget and area estimates for each space. This solution takes the form of a schematic diagram, showing without precise dimensions proposed relationships between areas and volumes based on the priorities of function, circulation, privacy, and acoustics. At this stage alternatives are often offered. For example, a client may want a marble bathroom floor, louvered vertical blinds, and a fabric covering for his living room walls, the costs of which exceed the budget. To resolve this, the designer might propose ceramic or vinyl asbestos tile, regular window shades, and painted walls, or, in new construction, a reduction in room size. In such proposals, costs can readily weight the alternatives.

If the program is satisfactory, the designer then goes ahead with the floor plan, elevations, and the architectural details. Lighting, colors, textures—applicable to floor, ceiling, and wallcoverings, and furnishings— are selected, and the arrangement of the latter and art objects completes

the design. The final presentation is made in whatever form seems clearest —perspective or isometric drawings or models—and should include necessary details, fabrics and other materials, color samples, and whatever is needed to give a complete visual idea.

The floor plan is drawn up according to square footage arrived at earlier, and space is allocated for each particular area. The plan is drawn with areas identified and the furniture arranged in groups on the basis of function, instead of as individual pieces.

A circulation layout will show all main or primary traffic patterns within each room, and between all adjoining areas, as well as secondary traffic patterns, planned so they do not conflict with the primary ones. Circulation in the home should stem from the entrance, with easy access to other areas. In public buildings, circulation should be easy from reception area to elevators, rest rooms, and whatever other areas are used by the public. Proper handling of traffic patterns in public buildings will also take into consideration privacy for executive offices.

FURNITURE SELECTION AND ARRANGEMENT

With the floor plan in hand, furniture arrangement is worked out. In doing so the designer keeps in mind how the empty spaces can be planned to increase interest in the functional spaces. He must also consider such things as allowing adequate space around certain kinds of equipment for their operation, leaving all pathways clear and doorways and passageways unobstructed. In general one strives to: (1) maintain a dominant center of interest; (2) balance spatial areas; (3) keep sizes in proper scale and proportion; (4) balance important pieces with others or with architectural elements such as doors or windows; (5) use only as many pieces as are needed; (6) place functional pieces where they can function easily; (7) keep furnishings simple; (8) manipulate visual space by use of mirrors, lighting, or wall treatment (directional designs, scenics, murals, etc.); (9) keep all passages clear; and (10) avoid sudden breaks in the continuity of the design. In the event that built-in and/or modular pieces, perhaps with interchangeable functions, offer the best design solution it becomes especially necessary to consider the plan of a space in relation to the height and the shape of the walls. In some contemporary interiors more than one level may be used—platforms, sunken seating areas, balconies—to provide extra sleep or work areas.

To determine the relationship between a piece of furniture, the arrangement of which it is part, and the space, the designer will experiment with rough sketches in order to achieve a pleasing design that encompasses the ideals of balance, good scale and proper proportion, and unity.

Color—of anything in the designed space (furniture, art objects, accessories, lighting fixtures, as well as all interior surfaces)—must be considered from the beginning of the planning. The subject is taken up separately in Chapter 5.

TYPICAL PLANNING PROBLEMS

The following examples illustrate the planning process for a residence, office, and school. In the case of the residence example, background material such as that given for the office and the school (both below) is provided in Chapter 13 (*The Dwelling*). The subsection *Designing*, given only for the residence, applies to both the office and school, and the *Programing* subsections given for the residence and office may be applied to the school.

A RESIDENCE

An eighty-year-old farm or suburban house (Fig. 4–1) is to be completely remodeled. The problem is to prepare a spatial arrangement for all interior functions, complete with furnishings. The exterior of the house is brick with openings that may be altered; it is desirable, however, to preserve the original character of the exterior. The house is to be occupied by a family of four with one child ten years old and one eight. In this example, both the floor plans (Fig. 4–2) and elevations (Fig. 4–3) for the first and second floors have been planned.

Programing

Activities and needs are listed for each of the general functions—living, eating, sleeping, and multipurpose—and might be broken down as follows (according to the tastes of the client):

A. *Living*

1. Seating for four to six people, with places for a larger number (without appearing overcrowded)

2. Accommodations for conversation for up to twelve people

3. Facilities for entertaining up to sixteen people

4–1 Hypothetical eighty-year-old suburban or farm house.

4. An atmosphere for listening to music

5. Soft, nonglare lighting, and task lighting

6. A fireplace, with seating for groups and storage space for wood

7. Ventilation and temperature control

8. Ready access to kitchen, view windows, and exterior terrace

9. Inconspicuous electrical outlets and equipment

B. *Eating*

1. Space and seating for normal dining for six

2. Flexible accommodations for buffet service for fifteen to twenty

3. Ready access to kitchen, outdoor dining, entry hall, and lavatory

4. View to south, east, or north

5. Speakers (from radio or record player)

6. Low ceiling

7. Emphasis on natural materials, such as in wood floors, trim, doors and windows, wood paneling, and in furniture

8. Lighting adequate for comfortable eating (which might include a dimmer)

9. Inconspicuous electrical outlets and equipment

10. Ventilation and temperature control

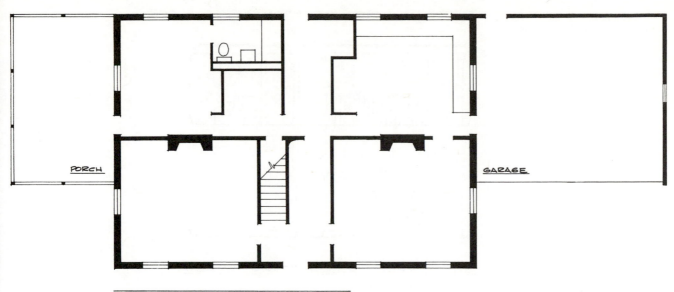

EXISTING LOWER FLOOR PLAN

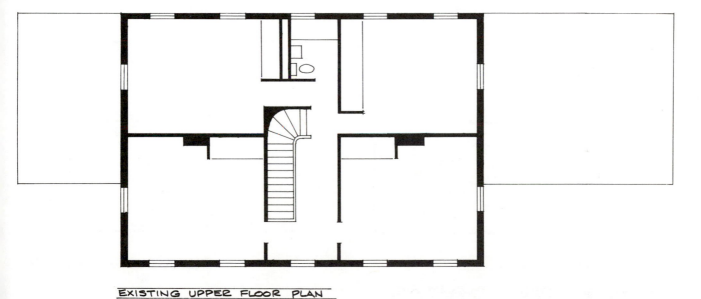

EXISTING UPPER FLOOR PLAN

C. Sleeping

1. Master bedroom with own bath and dressing room

2. Two additional bedrooms (sharing one bath)

3. Access to hall without need to pass through living room

4. Built-in storage, with drawers and shelves

5. Walk-in closets

6. Lighting for reading

7. Desk units

8. Ventilation and temperature control

4–2 Existing upper- and lower-floor plans of house shown in Fig. 4–1.

4–3   Existing upper- and lower-floor elevations of house shown in Fig. 4–1.

ENTRY HALL SIDE ELEVATION - UPPER FLOOR

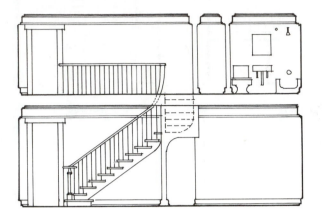

ENTRY HALL SIDE ELEVATION - LOWER FLOOR

EXISTING   INTERIOR   ELEVATIONS

SIDE WALL - UPPER FLOOR   END WALL - UPPER FLOOR

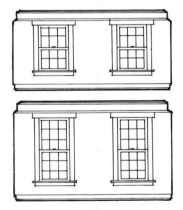

SIDE WALL - LOWER FLOOR   END WALL - LOWER FLOOR

EXISTING   INTERIOR   ELEVATIONS

9. Soundproofing between rooms

10. Windows placed to avoid morning light

11. Inconspicuous electrical outlets and equipment

D. *Multipurpose* (*entertainment and play*)

1. Ready access to the hall and lavatory

2. Space and facilities for games such as ping-pong, cards

3. Sound system

4. Space for dancing

5. Accommodations for conversation

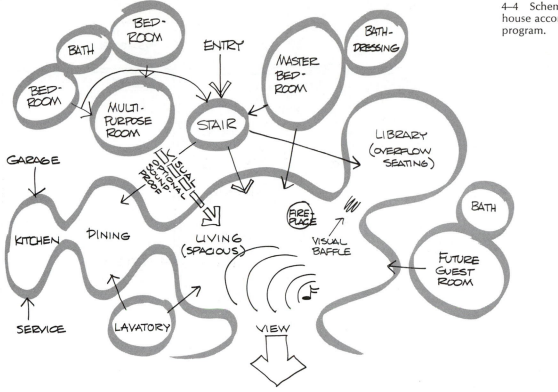

4–4 Schematic diagram of house according to planning program.

Designing

The designing phase has the following steps:

1. Schematic diagrams (Fig. 4–4) to show roughly the information gathered in the programing combined with spatial requirements for all activities, circulation, and furniture groups.

2. Design sketches (Fig. 4–5) that conform to and amplify the schematic diagram (Fig. 4–4) are worked out concurrently with rough perspectives (Figs. 4–6 and 4–7) or models to show the character, size, and scale of the space and to illustrate the transitional experience of a person moving from space to space. Perspective charts ("underlays") are often used for this part of the program.

3. Rough sketches of detail elements (Fig. 4–8)—windows, doors, and woodwork or any built-ins such as storage walls, fireplaces, hardware, railings, stairs, and areas for planting—are then made.

4. After tentative decisions about color have been made, preliminary shopping for furniture, fabrics, rugs, lighting fixtures, and decorative objects (at showrooms or through catalogs) is done.

5. Tentative selection of the items shopped is made from whatever has been gathered—samples, photographs, sketches, and specifications.

6. Evaluation of all material and design as they relate to the original program is done. If preliminary designs are satisfactory, final drawings (Figs. 4–9—12) are prepared and final furnishings selected after approval of product.

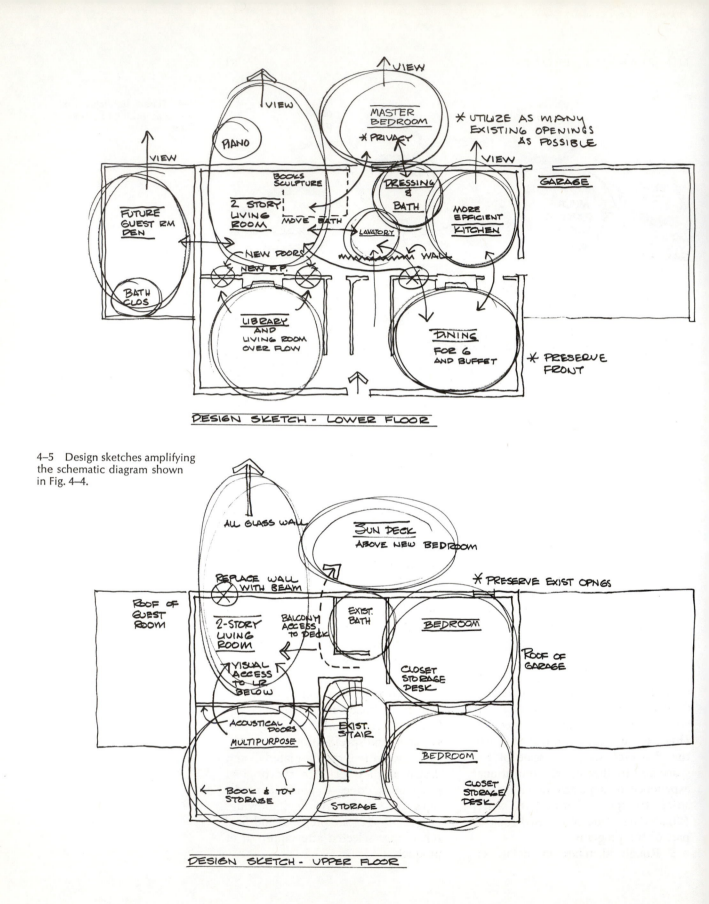

DESIGN SKETCH - LOWER FLOOR

Labels within lower floor sketch:

VIEW

VIEW

VIEW

MASTER BEDROOM
* PRIVACY

* UTILIZE AS MANY EXISTING OPENINGS AS POSSIBLE

GARAGE

PIANO

BOOKS SCULPTURE

DRESSING & BATH

MORE EFFICIENT KITCHEN

2 STORY LIVING ROOM

MOVE BATH

LAVATORY

FUTURE GUEST RM DEN

NEW DOORS

NEW F.P.

WAVE WALL

BATH CLOS

LIBRARY AND LIVING ROOM OVER FLOW

DINING FOR 6 AND BUFFET

* PRESERVE FRONT

4–5 Design sketches amplifying the schematic diagram shown in Fig. 4–4.

DESIGN SKETCH - UPPER FLOOR

Labels within upper floor sketch:

ALL GLASS WALL

SUN DECK
ABOVE NEW BEDROOM

* PRESERVE EXIST OPNGS

REPLACE WALL WITH BEAM

ROOF OF GUEST ROOM

2-STORY LIVING ROOM

BALCONY ACCESS TO DECK

EXIST. BATH

BEDROOM

CLOSET STORAGE DESK

ROOF OF GARAGE

VISUAL ACCESS TO LR BELOW

ACOUSTICAL DOORS

MULTIPURPOSE

EXIST. STAIR

BEDROOM

CLOSET STORAGE DESK

BOOK & TOY STORAGE

STORAGE

4–6 *Above,* rough perspective of entrance hall. (Note inviting character of openings at end of hall to left and right.) *Below,* perspective of opening to left.

4–7   *Above,* rough perspective
of double-height living space.
Wall continued beyond
windows increases sense of
space in interior and enhances
privacy. *Below,* perspective
of living space in direction
opposite that of view above.
Fireplace divides formal and
intimate seating spaces, and
multipurpose room is on upper
level.

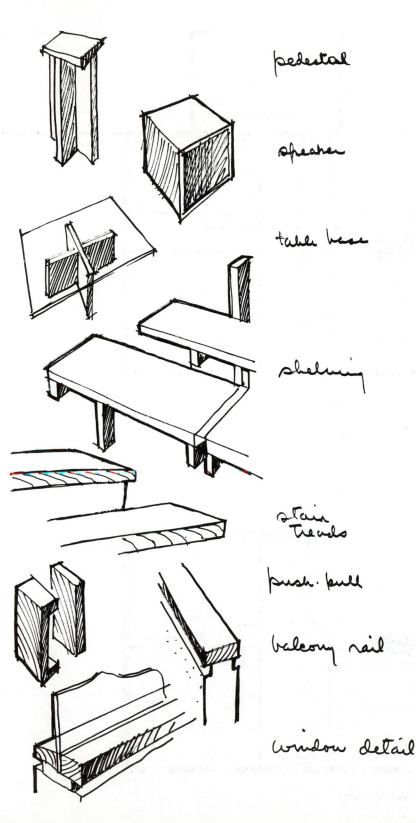

4–8 Sketches of detail elements.

pedestal

speaker

table base

shelving

stair treads

push-pull

balcony rail

window detail

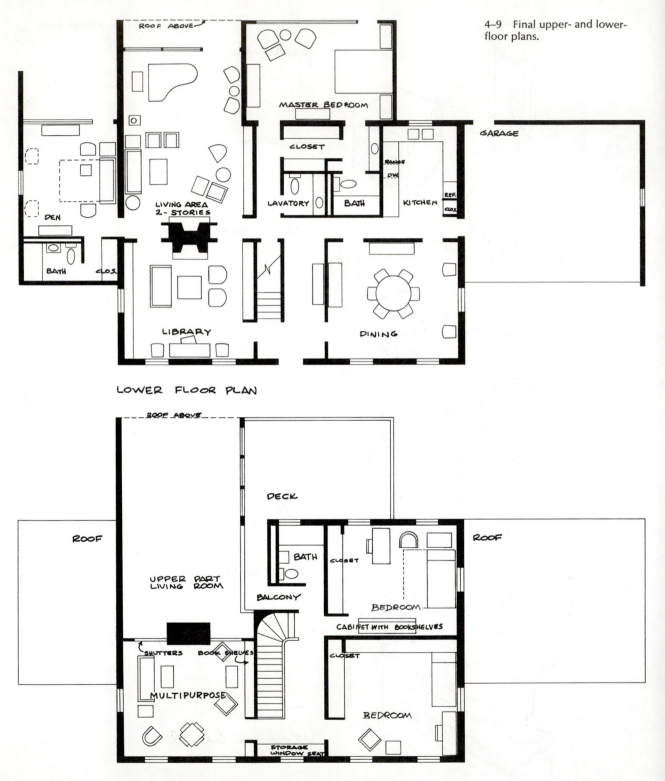

4–9 Final upper- and lower-floor plans.

LOWER FLOOR PLAN

UPPER FLOOR PLAN

4–10 Final drawings of entrance hall (*left*) and view to left from end of hall.

4–11   Final drawing of living
space.

4–12   Final lighting plan.

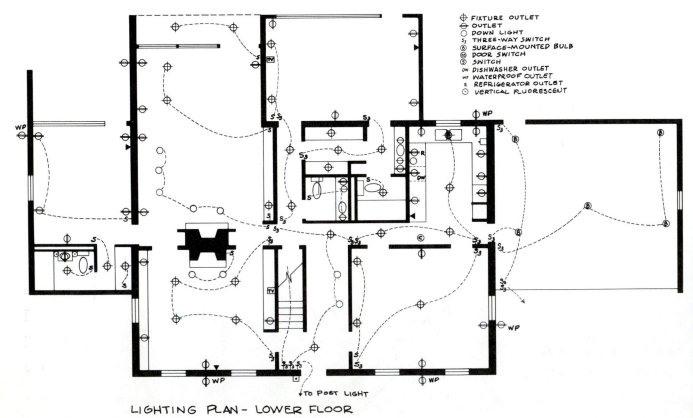

LIGHTING PLAN – LOWER FLOOR

AN OFFICE

An architectural firm has rented space in a new office building. The task is to solve all functional and esthetic problems and prepare complete design drawings.

The plan (Fig. 4–13) is typical of urban office structures, with open floor and windows around the perimeter and fixed elements such as elevators, stairs, and restrooms.

In this example the schematic diagram (Fig. 4–14), the design sketch (Fig. 4–15), and the final floor plan (Fig. 4–16) are shown.

Programing

Activities and needs are listed for each of the general functions—reception-waiting, conferences, principal offices (executive), secondary offices, drafting, model-making, library, and restrooms.[1] Each of these functions might be further broken down as in the following example:

A. *Reception Area*

1. Visibility from elevator

2. Seating for ten

3. Visual command of area by receptionist

4. Access to conference rooms and certain offices

5. Separation from offices

6. Access to toilets

1. Unlike the case with the residence, not all the activities or needs listed will be treated below.

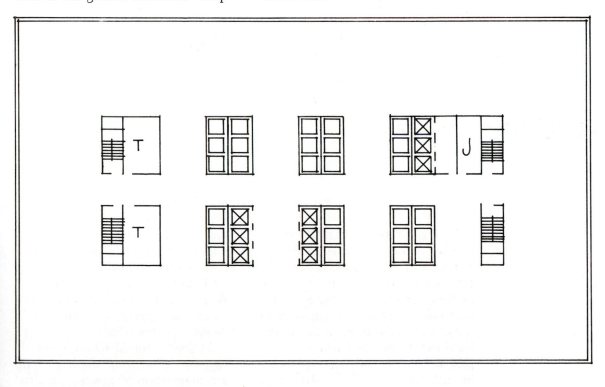

EXISTING FLOOR PLAN

4–13   Floor plan of existing office.

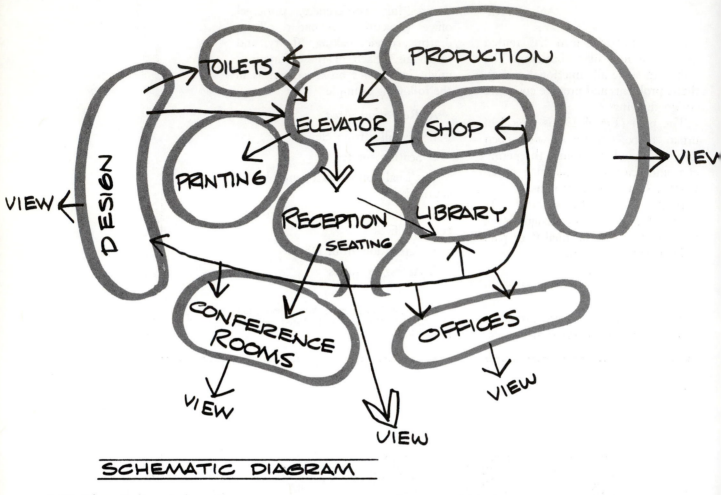

SCHEMATIC DIAGRAM

4–14 Schematic diagram of office according to planning program.

Background

Since the Second World War the number of large office buildings has increased at a phenomenal rate. In 1968 more than 70 percent of the working force in the United States were office workers. The approach to the office interior is unlike any other. Each individual office area is a complex mixture of varying ingredients in such things as the allotment of space, equipment required, fixtures and furnishings needed, and use of flexible partitions. A single space may enclose one to more than one hundred desks. The stratification of duties and responsibilities within an organization occupying the space is likely to have a complexity that is reflected in a variety of spaces that range from general work areas to individual private offices.

The main consideration in the design of commercial interiors is the accommodation of economy in structure with an attractive and healthful environment.

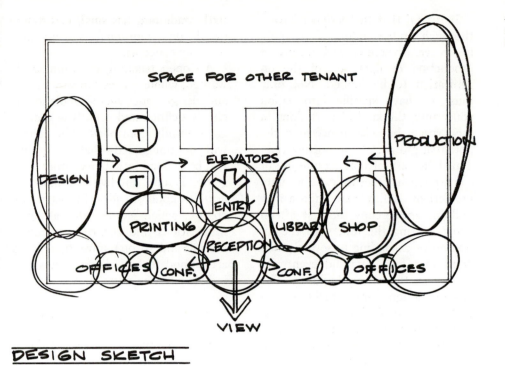

4–15 Design sketch amplifying schematic diagram shown in Fig. 4–14.

DESIGN SKETCH

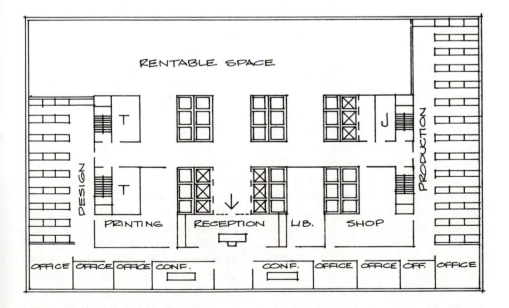

4–16 Final floor plan of office.

FINAL FLOOR PLAN

It is vital that the designer have a thorough understanding of the public image, structure, and means of production or operation of the organization to be housed. Not only must he have specific information concerning the kind of work done in each space, but also concerning the potential growth of the organization. This latter aspect may require use of a computer in order to make accurate predictions. A firm may build a new building and occupy the first fifteen floors, renting the rest, with the intention of expanding to several more floors in a few years and eventually occupying the entire building. The interior designer must make a plan that allows for flexibility to make expansion as economical as possible.

A job of this kind, today, can involve 800,000 square feet and twenty-four floors, as was the case with the General Motors Building in New York City. Planning on this scale covers offices that embrace every degree of privacy and status from the least important junior executive to the president, and hence vary greatly in size and requirements. It must also include work areas that hold, say, four persons to hundreds.

In addition to the requirements of space allotment, personnel distribution, and use of equipment, work area relationships that are peculiar to the commercial office are elements such as volume movement of people, elevator programing, storage, and the problems of cafeterias and rest areas.

A SCHOOL

A school board in a small city wishes to have an existing school building altered to meet the demands of modern teaching methods. The school includes kindergarten through sixth grade and has small classrooms based on traditional seating and teaching concepts.

An open teaching environment is wanted, where classes can vary in size and design, but where circulation is clearly defined and acoustical aspects are carefully controlled. The school will be nongraded—that is, groups will be defined by activity rather than grade. Hence, subdivisions must be flexible enough to allow for maximum change, which requires that all communications and services (air-conditioning and so on) must be able to accommodate both large groups and individual activities.

Background

New concepts of education developed in recent years have led to a total reevaluation of buildings used for education at all levels, from preschool to college. These radical changes demand a flexible school environment. Not many years ago the arrangement was static—rows of seats fastened to the floor, the teacher's desk in one spot, light from windows too high for the student to look out—and all school activities were based on the teacher at desk or blackboard, with students at blackboard or desk.

Today, with less emphasis on the acquisition of factual knowledge and more on developing the ability to think, to discriminate, and to evaluate and deal with ideas, instruction is becoming more a matter of *interaction* (of ideas and values) between student and teacher. Since the first requisite to this process is communication, it must also be the central consideration in the design of school buildings.

Flexibility is also a major requirement if the environment is to keep pace with the rapidly changing concepts of education and the new tools of education, which are being introduced constantly.

Teaching devices that particularly require flexibility are closed-circuit and educational television, film and audio equipment, and those devices based on the use of computers. Computers are also used for various administrative processes and for the scheduling of classes and the use of resources and facilities.

In school libraries much material formerly on shelves will be on microfilm; auditoriums will be designed for focusing attention of large groups without losing a desirable intimate quality.

Spaces for small- and large-group instruction are needed, and readily movable partitions are a particularly economical means of providing these. Partitions can be transparent (often recommended for administrative space), translucent, or opaque, and may be of several different materials. They can be made to fold away, slide (or coil) into a wall, or be shifted completely. They should be flame-resistant and nonglare and have good noise-damping properties. A kind appropriate to any need is available.

Provision should be made for expansion, and although economics may necessitate starting with minimal equipment, allowance for future wiring and operating facilities should be included in the original plan.

Fresh views of the outdoors are constructive in any interior space designed for educational purposes, as are strong, cheerful colors used in original ways, and the careful scaling of spaces and furnishings used by the students. On the other hand the designer must keep in mind that today's school buildings are also being used for community purposes. The days of monumental buildings, closed and dark when the students were not using them, are past. The new schools are much more than part-time shelters for instruction; they are becoming an important full-time part of city and town life.

BIBLIOGRAPHY

CAPELLE, FRIEDRICH W. *Professional Perspective Drawings for Architects and Engineers* (McGraw-Hill, 1961). A simplified, concise approach, with clearly explained formulas.

FRIEDMAN, ARNOLD; PILE, JOHN; AND WILSON, FORREST. *Interior Design, an Introduction to Architectural Interiors* (American Elsevier, 1970). Interesting discussion of the purpose of design. Excellent material on interior construction is emphatically technical.

GATZ, KONRAD. *Modern Architectural Detailing*, Vol. IV (Reinhold, 1969). Technical; useful to those focusing on details of design.

HOHAUSEN, SANFORD. *Architectural and Interior Models; Design and Construction* (Reinhold, 1970). Technical; everything one needs to know in making design models.

MARTIN, C. LESLIE. *Design Graphics* (Macmillan, 1962). Methods of drawing, drafting, and lettering beginning sketches to final presentation. Clear and comprehensive.

PICKERING, ERNEST. *Architectural Design* (Wiley, 1941). Excellent reference for architectural forms or design. Fine illustrations, both photographs and scaled drawings.

WILSON, JOSE, AND LEAMAN, ARTHUR. *Decorating Defined: A Dictionary of Decoration and Design* (Simon and Schuster, 1970). Definitions of 1400 terms used in connection with every aspect of interior design. Many well-chosen illustrations.

5

Pleasure in color is spontaneous. The joy people find in nature, in the colors of a sunset or a beautiful room, is deeply emotional and requires no effort or explanation. Color, like music, provokes many moods—cheer, excitement, tranquility (Figs. 5–1 and 5–2)—and no reasons for such reactions need be given here. Everyday expressions such as "feeling blue," "in the pink," and "seeing red," give evidence of the identification of certain colors with specific emotions. Yet, as with all aspects of esthetics, individual reactions to color vary greatly.

Color has long had a symbolic role in religion and magic. In early civilizations its use was limited, directed mainly by tradition or authority. This "classical" or symbolic tradition, in which color was rarely used as personal expression, may still be found in church ritual and in the conventions of heraldry.

The struggle for freedom of the human mind and spirit during the Renaissance inspired a change that was also reflected in the use of color, and with the invention of oil painting, the artist, designer, and decorator began to use color in more varied ways. In this tradition, the "creative" one, there was no question of compliance with ritual, and the artist or designer was expected to show originality and invention and express his individuality. Where the "classical" tradition used primary colors, the "creative" one invaded and exploited new regions of the spectrum, using colors such as purples, yellows, blue-greens, olives, and mauves. The contemporary Western world, particularly America, has been self-conscious about color, perhaps because of its puritanical origins. Where architecture and interiors in ancient Greece or Pompeii, for example, or in Renaissance Europe were bold with color (and brilliant colors are commonly used in Eastern countries such as Thailand), American taste in color has tended to be restrained. However, in recent years, in a freer and more prosperous society, this has been changing at a rapidly increasing rate.

COLOR

COLOR NOTATION

Color has three descriptive properties: *hue, value,* and *intensity* (also called *saturation* and *chroma*). Hue is simply the name of a color—red, blue, and so on. Value is the lightness or darkness of a color—that is, the amount of light the color reflects or transmits. A color of very high value may be almost white, and the darkest (lowest value) color will be almost black. (Color is, of course, a function of light. When all light is absorbed by a surface, the result is *black,* and when all light is reflected, the result is *white*; thus, without light there can be no color.) Intensity describes the strength or purity of the color—its apparent distance from a neutral gray: red has high intensity; rose has low intensity.

There are several color theories and systems of representation of color relationships. Some of the best known are the Prang, Ostwald, and Munsell. The Birren color circle (Fig. 5–3) from *The American Colorist* is used here. However, any system is only an aid and should be used with care and an understanding of its possibilities and limitations. The Munsell System is a very comprehensive one, unique in its color classification, and because of its potential in the precise identification of a color, especially useful to the interior designer. It is based on five principal hues and five intermediate ones: red and yellow-red; yellow and green-yellow; green and blue-green; blue and purple-blue; purple and red-purple. These are arranged on a three-dimensional structure in which value ranges on a vertical center axis from black at the bottom to white at the top. The hues are represented as radiating horizontally from the midpoint of the axis, with the intensity of the hues expressed as the distance from the vertical axis—the closer to it, the lower the intensity. Each color is shown as a square, where the three elements—hue, value, and intensity—theoretically intersect. Each square stands for one *and only one* color. The notation system uses letters and numerals, which indicate hue, value, and intensity: R 5/10 (or R 5-10) would be a red of medium value and high intensity.

COMMERCIAL DESIGNATIONS

Promotional color names—"shocking pink," for example, which has enjoyed a wide vogue—are of little use to the interior designer. The names identifying many paint colors, however, are relatively consistent and, hence, meaningful and useful. Table 5–1 lists some of these names with a brief and necessarily inexact description of the pigments and colors they represent.

The Intersociety Color Council, working with the National Bureau of Standards, has compiled *A Dictionary of Color Names*.[1] It has more than seven thousand color names, including the Munsell color notations, and is useful when problems arise concerning exact designations of color. Another useful reference is the *Color Harmony Manual*, and a supplement, *Descriptive Color Names Dictionary*, published by the Container Corporation of America.

EFFECT OF LIGHT SOURCE

All light sources have color. Natural light at dawn has a pink and orange glow, which shifts to yellow as the sun rises. At noon reflected light from the sky is white or pale blue. At sunset it becomes orange and pink. The average person is not conscious of the fact that the appearance of surfaces change as the light illuminating them changes. Incandescent

1. Available in many libraries and (as National Bureau of Standards Circular 553, 1955) from the U.S. Government Printing Office, Washington, D.C.

light has a mostly yellowish glow. Fluorescent light varies from pink to yellow to white to pale blue. At low levels of illumination most people find a warm tint (pink, orange, yellow) most pleasing—the mellow glow of firelight, candles, incandescent bulbs. Dim light used with warm colors gives an intimate, friendly atmosphere, flatters the complexion, and provides the environment conducive to rest and relaxation. Bluish or greenish tints in low illumination make people appear pallid, while under high levels of illumination, whiter and cooler lights give them a more natural appearance, which is excellent for working environments.

A white handkerchief taken from a sunny yard into a dimly lit room will still look white, not gray. While the constancy of white holds under all light intensities, this is not true of colors, which tend to wash out or grow dull in low illumination. As light dims, medium- and low-value colors tend to become indistinguishable, and certain hues are seen as gray sooner than others: blue, for example, before yellow, the latter the last color to remain distinguishable as illumination decreases.

RELATIVE COLOR EFFECTS

A person with normal vision can discriminate at least two thousand colors, and, although the experience of color can be highly subjective, there are definite laws that govern the effect (in terms of the viewer's experience) of one color on another. Thus, a color must always be evaluated or interpreted in relation to other colors. No one color is ever completely isolated from all others: a room that is totally white, for example, will be

Table 5–1. Common Pigment Colors

NAME	DESCRIPTION	INTENSITY*	VALUE*
Alizarin Crimson	Bright red	2	4
Geranium Lake	Bright pinkish red	1	3
Crimson Lake	Deep red, slightly blue	2	4
Carmine	Deep purple-red	1	4
Scarlet Lake	Bright red, slightly orange	1	3
Indian Red	Tawny red	4	4
Venetian Red	Orange-red	3	4
Light Red (English Red)	Yellow-red	2	3
Chinese Red	Yellow-red	3	3
Cadmium Orange	Deep orange	1	2
Chrome Yellow Deep	Orange-yellow	2	3
Cadmium Yellow Deep	Slightly orange-yellow	2	3
Gamboge	Reddish yellow	2	2
Chrome Yellow Medium	Toward lemon-yellow	3	2
Cadmium Yellow Medium	Deep lemon-yellow	3	2
Cadmium Yellow Light	Light lemon-yellow	4	1
Lemon Yellow	——	2	1
Sap Green	Yellow-green	3	3
Chrome Green	Slightly yellow-green	3	3
Olive Green	Grayed yellow-green	4	3
Viridian	Bright blue-green	3	3
Cobalt Blue	Bright sky blue	2	3
Ultramarine	Darker than cobalt blue	2	4
Prussian Blue	Deep blue	2	4
Indigo	Purple-blue	4	4
Mauve	Light purple	2	3
Sepia	Grayed red-yellow brown	4	4
Burnt Sienna	Red-brown	–	3
Vandyke Brown	Red-brown	4	4
Raw Umber	Reddish yellow-brown	4	4
Burnt Umber	Yellow-brown	–	3
Raw Sienna	Yellow-brown	–	3
Charcoal Gray	Dark warm gray, almost black	–	5
Payne's Gray	Deep gray with blue cast	–	4
Neutral Tint	Deep gray with slight purple cast	–	4

* Numbers indicate: 1, very high; 2, high; 3, medium; 4, low; and 5, very low.

seen in relation to anyone occupying it—in relation, that is, to his skin tone or clothing. A white panel next to a red one will tend to look cool—slightly greenish—because the "after-image" (a kind of negative impression that the eye retains briefly after one has looked at anything) of a color is its complement. Hence, a color must be considered in relation to any other colors in any successful design. (Creating a color chart is an exercise that will show the beginner clearly how one color affects another, whether mixed with it or placed next to it. Figure 5–3 indicates how to go about this.)

COLOR SCHEMES

Color "schemes" are generally either related schemes, which are based on likeness, or complementary, based on contrast. Related schemes, commonly used in interiors, are monochromatic or analogous. A monochromatic scheme (Fig. 5–4) is based on two or more variations of the same hue—for example, a carpet of deep blue-green, furniture a lighter value, and walls a third. An analogous scheme (Fig. 5–5) uses colors that are adjacent in the spectrum and have one hue in common. Thus, an analogous scheme might consist of all hues from yellow through green to, but not including, blue. An illustration of this kind of scheme in nature is the colors one sees in the depths of clear ocean water.

Complementary schemes, based on contrast, are stimulating. Nature uses many complementary schemes, such as touches of orange or yellow often found with blue on birds or butterflies. The simple complementary

scheme (Fig. 5–6) is based on opposites (complements) on the color chart. The opposites involving the primary colors—yellow and violet, red and green, orange and blue—offer greater contrast than do opposites of intermediate hues such as yellow-orange or blue-violet. When hues are paired exactly, the results are usually effective. Since hues of the same value placed together can dazzle the eye, it is usually better to make one color of the pair a different value. The double- or split-complementary scheme (Fig. 5–7) combines analogous hues (above) with the complement of one of them; that is, one hue is usually combined with the two hues that lie adjacent to its complement—for example, yellow with red-violet and blue-violet, or red with yellow-green and blue-green. Split-complement schemes require more care than related ones, but may be more visually interesting. In this kind of a scheme, the key color should be the purest.

Triad color schemes (Fig. 5–8) consist of hues four steps apart and equidistant from each other on the chart. A combination of primary colors such as red, yellow, and blue is elementary in its appeal. The triad of orange, green, and violet is considerably more interesting and subtle, while the triad of red-violet, yellow-orange, and blue-green is more exotic.

While all the hues may be used at one time, such broad use requires some planned control; for example, the major colors might be predominantly warm or predominantly cool; the different hues could be featured in a number of intensities—the same for each hue. In designing for the individual, of course, client color preferences must be the primary determinant, except where the designer

5–1 Color lends cheerfulness to a modern kitchen.

5–2 An interior in which tranquility is largely attributable to the colors used.

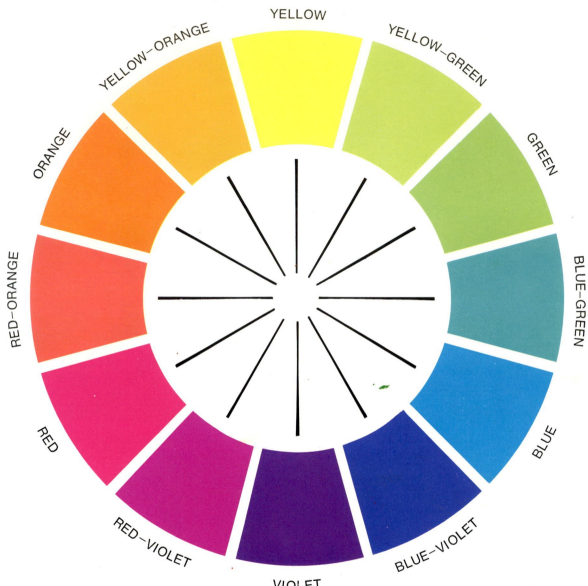

YELLOW

YELLOW–ORANGE

YELLOW–GREEN

ORANGE

GREEN

RED–ORANGE

BLUE–GREEN

RED

BLUE

RED–VIOLET

BLUE–VIOLET

VIOLET

5–3   The Birren color chart. The primary colors are yellow, blue, and red. The secondary colors are made from equal parts of any two primaries—green from yellow and blue, violet from blue and red, and orange from red and yellow. The complement of a color is the color opposite it on the chart. Complements used together offer the greatest contrast; when mixed they neutralize and gray each other. (Theoretically a true gray is made from equal parts of the three primary colors; pigments, however, are not always true.) All remaining colors (those between the primary and secondary ones, called tertiary) are made by mixing the colors adjacent to them on the circle; for example, red and orange give the tertiary red-orange.

5–4 A monochromatic color scheme.

5–5 An analogous color scheme.

5–6 A simple complementary color scheme.

5–7 An adaptation of a
double- or split-complementary
color scheme.

5–8 An adaptation of a triad
color scheme.

5–9 Soft colors used in a room that has relatively large expanses of uninterrupted surface.

5–10 Warm colors invest a room with a sense of excitement.

5–11 Cool colors in conjunction with simple forms create a tranquil space.

5–12 Medium values dominate in the large spaces of a general office.

5–13 Colors in a private office are of greater variety and higher value than those in a general office.

5–14 Simple, essentially primary colors in an elementary-grade classroom.

5–15 Blue and red dominate in a store interior.

5–16 Warm colors in a modern restaurant.

anticipates some objectionable result of the client's choice.

Color planning should, where feasible, be in terms of a whole unit—house, apartment, office, factory, and so on. Any two adjoining rooms should harmonize and all the rooms should be related. Balance should be a consideration, with color areas and values planned in relation to each space, shape and placement of each piece of furniture, and all patterns or textures. Generally, large areas are better in soft (low-intensity) colors (Fig. 5–9), with bright colors used most effectively for accents and smaller areas. Unity can be assured by relating the colors to whatever it is in the planning space that constitutes the key to the scheme. With this in mind, colors should be selected first for the background (floors, walls, and ceilings), then for draperies and larger furniture pieces, and, finally, accents.

Colors of middle or low values appear much stronger in a large area than in a small sample, and very light colors have the opposite effect, appearing lighter in a large area. Hence, all paint samples on a wall should occupy an area of at least two square feet, and should be tried in different lights—on a window wall, for example, as well as on a wall opposite, and so on.

EMOTIONAL AND SPATIAL EFFECTS

Certain useful generalities can be made about the optical and emotional effects of color. A main distinction is the one between colors that give a sense of warmth and those that give a sense of coolness. The warm hues shown in the Birren circle (Fig. 5–3) are red, red-orange, orange, yellow-orange, and yellow; the cool hues are green, green-blue, blue, blue-violet, and violet. Yellow-green and red-violet stand at dividing points and seem to blend warmth and coolness. Warm colors seem to advance, and certain of these—red, red-orange, and orange—have been shown in clinical studies to produce in most people impulsiveness and a sense of excitement (Fig. 5–10). Blood pressure and pulse in persons viewing warm colors tend to be higher than in those viewing cool colors, and attention goes outward. Cool hues seem to recede, and people generally react to them in a passive way (Fig. 5–11). Green and blue offer the greatest sense of tranquility, and yellow, a sense of cheerfulness. Because of the optical illusion (of advancing and receding colors) the apparent size and shape of areas can be varied according to the colors used.

As indicated in Chapter 3, color can be one of the devices for achieving rhythmic effects (in a particular pattern or in the general design) through repetition or progression of hue, value, or intensity. In a similar manner emphasis and contrast can be produced or modified by the use of color, as can unity.

PRACTICAL APPLICATIONS OF COLOR

In the mid-twenties, for the first time, the use of color in environment was considered from a point of view other than esthetic. A great deal of research was done and techniques were worked out to measure eye fatigue in relation to color. At that time it was definitely determined that control of color in an interior had a vital bearing on human efficiency and well-being. Since that time the functional approach in the use of color has been increasing in importance. In many contemporary interiors function is considered ahead of appearance and it is given some consideration in almost all designs. This applies particularly to areas where groups of people work rather than relax. Color can play a functional role in a variety of cases; for example, to improve efficiency and morale in an office, to lower accident frequency in a factory, to aid psychotherapy or hospital convalescence, to create an appetizing environment where food is served, to help sell merchandise, and to win public approval of municipal projects presented in models.

IN BUSINESS OFFICES

Certain general recommendations can be made for planning the color of various kinds of facilities. An all-black interior is emotionally depressing. Riotous color in an interior can be similarly distressing and even exhausting. Ideal colors for general offices are white or off-white for the ceiling, or overhead, with wall colors a medium value, such as beige, oyster white, or aqua (Fig. 5–12). The eye tends to be attracted to large white areas, and pure white is undesirable for walls because it causes the pupil to contract, creating glare, fogging vision, and thus fatiguing the eye, with consequent impairment of efficiency. Floors, equipment, and furniture should be medium value or lighter. To add interest and variation, fairly high-intensity colors can be used for upholstery. Because the human eye adjusts quickly to brightness and slowly to darkness, a dark work area surrounded by bright or white walls makes a task more difficult. Thus, a task area should be well lighted and light in tone, with walls, floor, and furnishings a slightly darker, but not dark, tone.

In private offices a wider variety of colors is acceptable (Fig. 5–13). Here one wall in a contrasting color, wood paneled, or with a textured wall covering is effective and practical. Deep colors on window walls are likely to cause too much contrast with daylight. Corridors and stairways adjacent to these offices may be related in complementary colors.

IN INDUSTRIAL SETTINGS

In industry, in the past, the main concern in selecting colors was practicality or durability. Today, designers are working to create, together with good visibility, a more comfortable and efficient environment, and to add enough interest to avoid monotony. Color can play a major role in achieving these ends.

Yellow is good for huge industrial interiors, giving a feeling of sunniness and decreasing the vaultlike quality of the room. High roof decks, trusses, and steelwork should be white or light gray for good light reflection; color overhead quenches light and distracts the eye. Hazardous and dangerous objects or areas should be clearly marked in vivid colors: yellow with black for strike-against, stumbling, and falling hazards; brilliant orange for the acute hazards likely to cut, crush, burn, or shock; and red for fire-protection devices. Containers for first-aid equipment should be green.

IN SCHOOLS

Basic color problems in schools are similar to those in other fields where groups of people work together. Efficient and comfortable visibility are necessary, plus any psychological color benefits that make learning easier or provide emotional relief. Ample light and minimum glare, with fairly uniform values of brightness in the field of view, are essential both psychologically and physically. Simple, basically primary colors tend to be good for elementary-grade classrooms (Fig. 5–14). In kindergartens a different color on each wall can be effective. A bright, cheerful room draws attention to itself, helping to release inner tensions. Good playroom colors are soft yellow, coral, or orange, stimulating outward action. In study rooms, muted tones of green, aqua, or beige are appropriate and functional. A different wall color can be used at the front of classrooms. Medium shades that harmonize with colors already chosen will help set off the instruction area and any lessons that are displayed.

IN HOSPITALS

In hospitals, color plans should be concerned almost entirely with function. Recent research permits a number of general conclusions. Clinical psychologists find that certain warm colors are diverting and tend to direct attention outward, a characteristic that can help relieve psychic tension. In operating rooms the glare of artificial lighting of high intensity has been largely overcome by using grayed green on walls and equipment, for the operating gowns and on sheets and towels. As the complement of human blood and tissue, it helps to keep the surgeon's vision acute.

IN THEATERS

In theaters, if medium or deep colors are used on walls, they should be contrasted with light colors on ceiling, architectural elements, floors, and furnishings to keep the eye from getting lost in the darker areas. White is especially disturbing when used near a stage. If one wall is to be a different color from the others, it is better if it is the rear wall or the area surrounding the stage.

IN HOTELS

Great variety should be avoided in buildings used by the general public, such as hotels and motels. Studies have shown that while a drab scheme may be emotionally depressing, a simple scheme composed of few colors has the broadest appeal. For the most part, it is safe to work with subtle variations of colors accented with stronger values of the same hues. (Orchid, lilac, and chartreuse rank low in color preference tests of occupants of hotels and motels, tending to give guests a sense of alienation.) Furnishings, carpeting, bedspreads, and curtains can be stronger tones of the hues used in painted areas, and corridors, washrooms, and alcoves can be painted in strong tones of warm colors.

IN SHOPS AND STORES

Color use recommended for hotels and motels generally also applies to shops and stores. Psychologically, the best colors are blue, red, and green, with yellow also acceptable for its high visibility (Fig. 5–15).

Off-white is a practical and satisfactory color for stores; good for major walls and for most ceilings, combined with more vivid colors for wall sections, alcoves, counters, displays, and free-standing columns. Bright yellow is good for areas at the end of a store furthest from the entrance, around elevators, and to stimulate impulse buying. Its high visibility helps to pull traffic in its direction.

IN EATING PLACES

Because warm colors tend to stimulate the appetite, ideal wall colors for eating places are yellow and orange (Fig. 5–16). A cocktail lounge and other such areas where illumination is normally low can be red or even a vivid orange.

BIBLIOGRAPHY

BIRREN, FABER. *Color for Interiors* (Whitney, 1963). Color as used in interiors from early ages to the present.
————. *Color Psychology and Color Therapy* (University Books, 1961). The psychology of color and the use in design of principles based on it.
HALSE, ALBERT O. *The Use of Color in Interiors* (McGraw-Hill, 1968). Authoritative, easy-to-use reference.
SLOANE, PATRICIA. *Color: Basic Principles and New Directions* (Reinhold, 1967). Changes in general attitudes to color today, possibly more useful to artists than designers.

6

Light is an environmental factor that affects every human being. Most important in the design of lighting are the people who will be using and moving through the lighted areas, and individual preferences vary in this matter as they do for all environmental elements. Older people, for example, prefer and often require more light than younger ones.

Any surface that is struck by light rays reflects some of that light. The brightness of the surface is a direct result of the amount of light reflected by that surface. Thus, a surface that reflects half the light that strikes it is said to have a reflectance of 50 percent. Any surface that reflects light is a source of illumination to other surfaces. Variations in reflectance are essential to visibility, providing one of the means necessary for distinguishing between objects. Glare is light in the wrong place, and usually occurs when the illumination source is small and/or not properly shielded. Bright light coming through a small window, for example, if viewed directly against the relatively dark wall, makes a

strong contrast between light and shadow, with resultant glare. A general rule concerning glare: the larger the area producing a given level of illumination, the lower the potential for glare. Where possible, large areas of low brightness are more desirable than small areas of high brightness. True quality lighting is achieved only when glare is eliminated.

The color of any part of an interior or of an object in it can be understood only in terms of the kind of light that illuminates it. Without light there is no color. As indicated in Chapter 5 (*Color*), light sources, although usually thought of as simply "white," have distinctive color: sunshine is warm, as is incandescent light; fluorescent light is generally cool. Thus, since colors selected under one light can appear very different when seen under another, it is essential to make such selections in the kind of light under which the colors will be used.

Since surfaces either absorb or reflect light, the degree of reflectance desired should also be considered in

LIGHTING AND LIGHTING

EQUIPMENT

the selection of color. A yellow surface, for example, will reflect most of the light from a yellow light source, and very little from a blue one. The reflectance of most neutral colors varies little with the light source, but highly intense colors show great variability according to source. In offices, schools, and industrial plants, reflectance has a definite effect on efficiency. Individual preferences can be given more weight where human activities are more varied and less concentrated, as in dwellings. Reflectances of common surface materials (available in chart form) vary from 6 percent to 82 percent.

DAYLIGHT

Daylight, the visible radiant energy of the sun, varies widely in color and intensity, and, hence, in psychological effect. Bright sunshine evokes cheerfulness; overcast, melancholy. On a clear, sunny day shadows are crisp and light intense and directional. On a hazy day shadows, if any,

are soft and the light seems to come from all directions. The use of daylight has distinct physical and economic as well as psychological advantages.

Recently developed methods [1] enable an architect or lighting consultant to predict accurately the amount of daylight that will be available at a particular location in an interior, providing a guide to the positioning and size of windows. This, in turn, enables the planning of interior lighting in a way that maximizes use of daylight and makes possible its proper integration with artificial light.

Light can be brought into an interior through windows at any level in a wall, through skylights or other openings, or by opening up an entire wall (Fig. 6–1). In the past, most walls were load-bearing and heavy, with window openings punched through for light and air. With today's construction methods (which do not require load-bearing walls), better window design, improved glass, and

1. From a study by Libbey-Owens-Ford Glass Company, Toledo, Ohio.

6–1   Windows augmented with
a skylight offer handsome
means of using daylight.

modern interior atmosphere control, daylight, which costs nothing, tends to be utilized for more and better natural lighting.

Variable light sources allow for flexibility, which can help satisfy some personal preferences and diminish the monotony of fixed lighting. Utilization of daylight, with its continuous shift in position and intensity, is one way to assure this variability. Uniform distribution of natural light can be achieved with multilateral daylighting, in which light comes from more than one level (Fig. 6–2).

Different functions in an interior require different kinds of light. For work such as painting or drafting, north light, which is shadow-free and most consistent, is best. Openings facing east or south will provide more direct and—as the sun moves across the sky—more dynamic lighting. Unless this lighting is carefully controlled by shading devices such as overhangs or blinds, problems arise from the harshness of the direct light of the sun. Venetian blinds are the most effective and flexible means of control, enabling the greatest use of illumination from the sky and admitting ground light while blocking out direct sunlight. Overhang arrangements, in addition to controlling direct sunlight, help keep rooms cooler in summer and do not interfere with ventilation. Where an overhang is used, the amount of daylight distributed within a room can be increased by use of high-reflectance materials on the ground adjacent to the window. The underside of overhangs should have a reflectance approximately that of the room ceiling.

Architects have long recognized the function of light in their designs; Frank Lloyd Wright made daylight an integral part of his, with heavy

6–2 Room with multilateral light source.

overhangs and cantilevered construction that created dramatic shadows at a low level. High clerestory windows gave an added dimension to the space and the forms within it, and small openings let the sun through in patterns without creating glare. He also used stained glass, with its pleasant effect of soft colors changing as the light moves.

ARTIFICIAL LIGHTING

Artificial lighting, which can be totally controlled, can stimulate activity and creativity or relaxation, change the nature of space, direct human movement, provide appropriate atmosphere, dramatize and silhouette forms, and enhance the richness of texture of interiors. Emphasis and excitement can be created by bright and focused lights, mystery through the use of dim or luminous ones, and decorative effects through strategic placement of colored light.

Light and color can be used as part of a background. They can be combined and directed from a variety of sources to create a purely decorative effect. Some feel that it is impossible to produce a distasteful effect with colored light; shocking, yes, or interesting, pleasing, subtle, or delicate, but always harmonious. (This is, of course, not the case with dyes or paints.) Colored light is becoming more important in providing decoration and atmosphere that can be controlled. It has been suggested that devices that project patterns of light could be used to create an interior environment in an undecorated space that could be easily changed when desired. Colored scenes are already being projected onto walls and ceilings to supply light, color, and decoration.

A light that produces full-spectrum illumination (Vita-lite [2]), duplicating natural light, includes ultraviolet radiation and is, therefore, germicidal and offers the other health-enhancing properties of natural light.

For any kind of artificial lighting, a lighting engineer is the specialist to be consulted, but as with all aspects

2. Duro-test Corporation, New York, N.Y.

of designing interior environment, some knowledge of systems and methods on the part of the designer will aid in making the right selection. Lighting should be considered from the beginning of any plan for an interior; it is generally agreed that lighting added to a plan and not part of it originally can destroy the effect of both the architectural space and the interior design.

The terms used to designate the elements that have been isolated from the total effect of natural light and utilized in lighting design are ambience, beam, focus, glitter, silhouette, and variety (Fig. 6–3). *Ambience* refers to an overall glow, with no concentrated, monodirectional source, that seems to fill a space and surround the persons or objects in it; a *beam* is a slender shaft of light from a concealed source; the *focus* is the point at which light is brightest; *glitter* is the sparkling effect of focusing a bright light on a reflecting surface (it can also be produced directly with tiny, clear, incandescent bulbs); *silhouette* is any form visible in outline only; and *variety* refers to shadows deliberately created in a lighted area in order to avoid monotony.

BASIC SYSTEMS

The basic systems of light make use of five kinds of light: direct, indirect, direct-indirect (or general diffuse), semidirect, and semi-indirect (Fig. 6–4). *Direct* light shines straight onto the object or area close to it, providing the sharpest contrast between light and dark (not always desirable) and making dramatic shadows. This kind of lighting produces glare if the units are not properly spaced or shielded. *Indirect* light is secondary

6–3 Some elements of artificial lighting—ambience, glitter, and silhouette—in settings of natural light.

DIRECT

INDIRECT

DIRECT
INDIRECT

SEMI-
DIRECT

SEMI-
INDIRECT

6–4 The five kinds of artificial-light distribution.

light, the result when light from an original source is thrown against another surface—usually ceiling or wall —from which it is reflected. In this case the ceiling or wall is part of the light source and its color is therefore a crucial element in the light produced. The diffuse quality of indirect light minimizes shadows and reflected glare. It is softer, less dramatic than direct light, and can be used for *general illumination*. *Direct-indirect* or *general diffuse* light uses both direct and indirect light distributed evenly in all directions. Any kind of fixture that has bulbs both inside and outside a reflector, as is frequently the case in table and floor lamps, produces diffused light. Shadows may be more noticeable and glare a problem if the

fixtures are not shielded. In *semi-direct* arrangements, 60–90 percent of the light is directed down to the work surface, with a small amount directed upward. *Semi-indirect* lighting directs 60–90 percent toward the ceiling and upper walls, using the ceiling as a main reflective source.

SOURCES

The two commonly used sources of artificial light in interiors are incandescent bulbs and fluorescent tubes (Fig. 6–5). Incandescent light is a concentrated source and can be directed easily to a point or area. The bulbs light instantly, give good color rendition, and are easy to maintain; they are, however, much more likely

to produce glare than fluorescent light and have a lower light output (relative to energy consumed) and shorter life, which make them more costly to operate than fluorescent lights. Because their fixtures are simpler and bulbs of different wattage can be used in the same socket, incandescent lighting is used more commonly in the home. There are three general categories of incandescent bulbs: general purpose (A and PS types), which are used in lamps and fixtures for general lighting and create a base or ambient level of illumination; reflector bulbs (PAR and R types), used for key or accent lighting (these have metal coating in the lower part that acts as a reflector); and decorative bulbs (C, FL, and G types), which are exposed light sources for chandeliers, sconces, and so on. All types are made in a wide variety of shapes and finishes, including frosting or coating to soften and diffuse the light and minimize glare.

Incandescent bulbs generally accentuate warm colors. Tinted bulbs, available in pink, blue, gold, or green, can be used to produce spatial effects —cooler and higher illumination giving a sense of greater space. Floodlights, which are made in many colors —pink, red, green-yellow, blue-white, blue, and amber—can be blended to create unusual and beautiful effects: pink and blue-white are complimentary to skin tones; yellow and amber can be combined to create an effect of sunshine; red, blue, and green are

6–5 Various forms of fluorescent (*a* to *d*) and incandescent (*e* to *l*) light sources: *a* is a standard fluorescent tube, *b* and *d*, "slim-line" type, and *c*, a "lumiline"; *e* is a flame-shape; *f*, *i*, and *k*, inside-frosted types; *g*, an "A" bulb; *h* and *j*, reflector types; and *l*, a showcase tube.

very strong, rarely used indoors, and are recommended only for spectacular effects.

The common fluorescent light is made only in tubular form, either straight or curved. A new U-shaped tube permits installation of supporting brackets at one end of the tube instead of both. The fixture used with this type of tube can thus have a more nearly square shape, making it particularly useful in modular designs. Because fluorescent installation requires more than the simple switch and socket of the incandescent light, its initial cost is higher. But the tubes last longer, are cooler, require (relative to light produced) fewer fixtures, and use less electricity than incandescents. Their greater efficiency and economy make them much more practical for schools, offices, and industrial and public buildings where high levels of general lighting are needed. Fluorescent light also diffuses more uniformly and provides more comfortable seeing conditions, reducing glare and shadows.

Fluorescent tubes are available in a range of shades that can be used to provide a cool or warm atmosphere and supply the right color tone for fabric, merchandise, or wall color. *Natural White* is generally preferred for store applications. It provides more red than most fluorescent and flatters complexions. *Warm White* creates a warm atmosphere and is close in color to the light of an incandescent bulb. It makes reds and yellows warm and bright, brings out the yellow in green, adds a warm tone to blue. Its light appears yellower at lower levels of illumination. *Deluxe Warm White* has a beige cast that is warmer than Warm White, brightens reds and yellows, and darkens blues

and greens. It blends well with incandescent light. *Cool White* produces a cool, neutral light with a blue-gray cast. *Deluxe Cool White* is similar, but has a red element added that improves the appearance of reds. It has little distortion but tends to gray colors slightly. *White* has a yellowish cast and accentuates yellows, yellow-greens, and orange. It strengthens tans, pinks, and greens, but will gray blues. *Soft White* has a pink cast and clarifies and brightens some pinks, reds, and tans. It is somewhat flattering to the complexion but dulls yellows and grays greens. *Daylight* has a blue cast similar to north light or natural daylight. It makes blues and greens bright and clear, and tends to gray reds, yellows, and orange. It is not flattering to the complexion. Colored fluorescents—blue, green, yellow, gold, pink, and rose—are useful for dramatic display effects. Near ultraviolet can be used for black-light applications, and "color rendition" fluorescents practically duplicate daylight.

Neon lights, also generally tubular, emit colored light and have applications similar to those of colored fluorescents.

Another light source, "high-intensity discharge" lights, is generally used commercially and out-of-doors, although it has a potential for interior use.

BRIGHTNESS

Artificial light can be produced at three levels of brightness—high, low, and glitter. High brightness usually comes from one or more exposed sources—incandescent, fluorescent, or both. Focus and the avoidance of glare are difficult with high brightness, which sometimes seems to fragment architectural space, the eye seeing the resultant harsh lights and darks (shadows) as additional forms in the design. Low brightness comes from one or more concealed sources and illuminates without the distraction inherent in exposed sources. The greater the number of concealed sources, the greater the interest and drama that will be produced. Glitter is produced by the use of many exposed individual point (small, sharply defined) sources of low brightness and may be direct or indirect. It has the excitement that bright light without glare has, and can create a gay atmosphere in interior space. Dimmer controls offer a means of combining different levels of illumination for a variety of effects.

LUMINAIRES

A luminaire is the combined assembly of lighting fixture and light source. Luminaires that can be seen should be selected for appearance as well as function, should control and direct light, shield it if required, and spread it over a surface large enough to make it visually comfortable. An exposed luminaire should function in a design even when not lighted. Luminaires are available in a wide variety of designs, from copies of medieval candelabra to abstract forms. Some contemporary styles use special low-glare bulbs, unshielded, as part of the fixture designs.

Luminaires (Fig. 6–6) are generally either recessed, surfaced-mounted, or pendant (suspended). Recessed luminaires are installed inside a ceiling or wall and have their openings flush with the surface. In addition to the housing (in effect, a metal can or box) and bulb, they may contain a reflector and shielding. Incandescent housings usually accommodate only

6–6 Recessed (*left*) and suspended luminaires (*below*).

one bulb and are often round in their exposed portion, which generally has an area of less than one square foot. Fluorescent housings are commonly rectangular and use a double row of lamps. The reflectors are flat metal or plastic sheets. (Shallow reflectors spread light in a wide pattern; deep ones concentrate light in a small area.) Shielding devices include baffles—metal or plastic plates that shield the bulb from sight at a normal viewing angle; louvers—shutterlike leaves of metal or plastic, parallel or in various patterns such as hexagons, circles, or squares, and usually painted white; lenses—molded glass or plastic that softens and redirects light by refraction; diffusers—glass, metal, or plastic grids or gratings that scatter the light.

Surface luminaires may be of the following kinds: general-diffusing, partial down-lighting, or directional down-lighting. For general diffusing, the light source (bulbs or tubes) should not be seen through or over the fixture. Surface luminaires are usually attached to the ceiling or high on a wall and include the following types: *cornice* (shielded by a horizontal recess, distributes light upward, downward along the wall, or both, giving dramatic interest to wallcoverings, draperies, color, or texture); *cove* (shielded by a horizontal recess, distributes soft, uniform, unemphatic light over ceiling—best when light-colored—and upper wall); and *soffit* (mounted on undersides of an architectural element such as an arch or lintel, can provide high level of light directly below, hence useful in bathrooms and kitchens). Recessed luminaires include the following types: *troffer* (usually with opening flush with ceiling); *luminous ceiling* (ceiling area lighting system comprising a continuous surface of transmitting

material of a diffusing or light-controlling character, with light sources mounted above it); and *luminous wall* (same as luminous ceiling but installed in wall).

Pendant or suspended luminaires with general-diffusing qualities also may provide partial down-lighting and usually are used decoratively. They hang from the ceiling and should be in harmony with the design scheme whether lighted or not. In selecting pendant luminaires one should consider how they will appear against a dark wall when lighted and against a light wall by daylight. When hung low enough to be in the direct line of sight, their brightness should be low. Direct-indirect pendant luminaires contribute to room lighting through their upward light and provide functional down-lighting. Luminaires with direct down-lighting are usually hung on or below eye level and have a sharp beam that produces definite shadow patterns. With those in which bulbs are exposed (usually for sparkle or accent, rather than illumination), additional lighting is usually needed. Because of the brilliance of clear bulbs, such fixtures should be mounted above the line of sight.

Table and floor lamps (Fig. 6–7) that are movable are still widely used and serve the same purpose that they have for centuries. As with all elements of a design, lamps should be both attractive and functional. It is particularly important that base and shade have a harmonious, integral relationship. Shades, opaque or translucent, are made of many materials: leather; parchment (more commonly an imitation); decorated paper; heavy paper laminated with sheets of other materials such as gold, silver, or tortoise shell; fabrics; and metals.

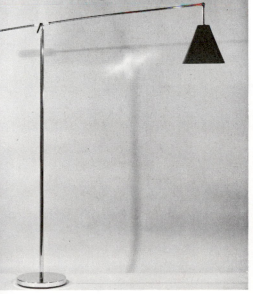

6–7 Table and floor lamps.

SWITCHES AND OUTLETS

Switches and outlets are an essential part of the lighting plan and locations should be worked out at the beginning of planning in relation to function of lighting and the activities that will take place in the space. Unless some light enters it from an adjoining space, each distinct space needs a light switch near its entrance.

Convenience is the keynote in location of switches: stairs and halls should have two-station switches; the switch on a bed lamp should be easy for a person to reach while lying down; switches in closet door frames can turn lights on and off with the movement of the door. Outlets should also be located conveniently and, as far as possible, so that they will be concealed by furniture.

6–8 General, task, and accent lighting in an office-industrial setting (*opposite*) and in a home. General lighting is provided in both cases by recessed ceiling lights. Task lighting is clearly seen in the blueprint area of the office, and illumination of the art objects in the home setting demonstrates accent lighting.

BASIC FUNCTIONS

Artificial light has three basic functions: general illumination, task lighting, and accent lighting (Fig. 6–8). General illumination should create a comfortable "seeing" environment and provide a substantially uniform level of illumination in an area. It is softer and less direct than task lighting, which illuminates relatively small areas, focusing special light on small, defined spaces. Close-work areas of most kinds—mirrors, where one needs a close-up view, desks, reading areas—require task lighting. Accent lighting, which includes the various kinds of spot lighting, focuses interest in a space by directing illumination onto it. It can confer visual drama, feature a work of art, or define a display; it is basically decorative. In the designs of today, lights that perform three functions individually are combined to create a variety of effects.

SPECIFIC APPLICATIONS

In planning lighting for any interior one must determine several things: first, the function of the area to be illuminated and, hence, the illumination requirements; second, whether it will be useful or necessary to integrate artificial with natural light and, if so, how; third, which kind of light —general, task, or accent—should predominate; fourth, which luminaires will best answer the needs determined above. In all determinations, the quality of light should be considered before the quantity. The success of any lighting is determined by the visual comfort of those using the space illuminated. Visual comfort requires that the illuminated area be free of shadows and reflections and that the illumination be neither distractingly dim nor bright.

COMMERCIAL AND INDUSTRIAL

Lighting for commercial offices as well as industrial facilities has an economic importance in that it can be directly related to the performance of the people working in them. General lighting for such areas should be relatively uniform, with special fixtures for task lighting.

General office lighting (Fig. 6–9) requires a high degree of flexibility because of the large number of different tasks performed in offices and in order to accommodate frequent changes in routine and personnel. There are several kinds of fixtures suitable for offices, all of which supply pleasant, evenly distributed light.

In selecting fixtures the cost to be considered should include not only the fixture, but also the installation, plus the maintenance and operating costs. (The higher initial cost of a better lamp or luminaire is often offset over the years by substantial savings in maintenance costs.) A lighting consultant can provide the information needed to determine costs.

Fixtures found in offices are almost always one (or more) of four types: pendant (usually fluorescent), surface-mounted, troffer, and luminous ceiling. Pendant types are used in older buildings where ceilings are high and service equipment such as pipes and ductwork are attached to the ceiling. These fixtures may be direct, indirect, or both and have the visual effect of lowering the ceiling and making ceiling clutter less noticeable. Surface-mounted fixtures are often used where ceilings are low, to provide direct or (when luminous side panels are used) semidirect lighting. They are used either individually or in tandem to form a row. Troffers can be installed in continuous or interrupted rows. Care should be taken to avoid great contrast between the color of the fixture and that of the ceiling color. Luminous ceilings may cover an entire area or may be used as panels in one portion of an area. In either case solid sheets of translucent plastic, many forms of louvering, or glass or plastic lenses may be used to conceal the fixture. A luminous ceiling provides a feeling of spaciousness; the newest combine excellent lighting with acoustical control and draft-free heating and cooling.

Small and private offices require a variety of lighting for the most demanding kind of paper work as well as for casual conversation. Since small rooms utilize light less efficiently than

6–9 Typical lighting for a general (*above*) and private (*left*) office. Lighting in the general office employs troffers.

large ones, they require more luminaires per unit area to achieve the same illumination level. Good quality lighting of a work surface necessitates two or more rows of luminaires.

STORES

The successfulness of store lighting for a large department store (Fig. 6–10) or a small specialty shop is measured by its effectiveness in selling and displaying merchandise. Good, strong lighting assures easy visibility and freshens color. Brightness can vary to focus attention in some areas and to minimize distraction in others. The three kinds of lighting required in most store interiors are: general lighting, display lighting, and perimeter lighting.

Because no two stores have identical lighting needs, generalizations cannot be applied rigidly, and consultation with a lighting specialist is usually essential. General lighting must be of a level and quality permitting easy, accurate examination of items displayed; it will usually either parallel the layout of the merchandise with appropriate atmosphere lighting or provide uniform illumination throughout the sales area. Each of three different methods of merchandising requires different general lighting. *Self-service* requires high levels of well-diffused light of a quality that allows easy seeing from a distance of several feet; recessed troffers and luminous ceilings are well suited for this. In *semi-service*, which requires some sales people, directional lighting from louver-shielded fluorescent fixtures is effective. High-style specialty shops, where service is personal, re-

quire an atmosphere of luxury, which can be achieved by low-level, soft, and well-diffused general lighting (Fig. 6–10), with dramatic display lights illuminating the merchandise.

Display lighting should first capture the attention of the customer, then reveal the merchandise, emphasizing its best feature. In showcase and wall-case lighting, it is especially important to use the right color for the merchandise and to avoid distracting reflections. There should be little difference between the light at the bottom of the showcase and that at the top. For wall cases, a brightness twice that of the general lighting is recommended. There is no special need for shelf lighting of stacked merchandise such as towels and sheets, but glassware, small appliances, gifts, and so on should be lighted so that they can be seen clearly, without shadows. Featured displays can be dramatically illuminated with directional lighting that brings out form and texture. For supplementary lighting, valances may be used along wall racks or shelving; such lighting is also effective in attracting attention from a distance. Light should not shine directly on mirrors, but on the area where the shopper stands, and it should flatter the complexion.

Perimeter lighting can give a store a sense of spaciousness, and is achieved by lighting vertical surfaces, such as walls, that define the limits of the larger shopping areas. Such lighting can also create brightness patterns that complement and enhance the general design and layout of the store. Decorative wall washes from colored spots or floodlights can add to the drama and effectiveness of the display, but must be used in a way that does not compete with the visual attractiveness of the goods.

6–10 Store lighting that offers easy visibility with variety.

SCHOOLS

Basic considerations required for satisfactory seeing in schools are similar to those for offices, and the types of luminaires used can be the same. A fluorescent system is usually most practical for a classroom. Since individual students may be performing different tasks, it is impractical to light a classroom only to the level needed for one task; hence, the general level should be designed for the task requiring the highest level. Special-purpose classrooms usually need special lighting: in shop, sewing, and art rooms, lighting should be planned on a specific-task basis. Rooms where art is taught should have luminaires whose light adds as little as possible to color. (The improved "color rendition" fluorescent is good for this purpose.) White chalk used on a blackboard provides maximum contrast and is easy to see, but it can cause eyestrain. Boards of no more than 20 percent reflectance are in common use now and are easier on the eyes than older conventional blackboards but require additional illumination.

Two kinds of classroom lighting are needed for work and study; one for work done with the head up and the line of sight essentially horizontal, and one for work done with the head down (Fig. 6–11). Visual comfort—primarily the relation between the amount of light relative to the amount of glare—should be provided for. In classrooms used for viewing projected images—movies, slides, filmstrips, or TV—the area immediately around the screen should be kept as light as possible without causing the image on the screen to lose contrast.

Most school auditoriums are multi-purpose. Atmosphere lighting can be provided by luminous ceilings, cove lighting, or suspended indirect luminaires. Dimming controls are essential if levels of illumination are to vary with the use to which the auditorium is put. Supplementary illumination is required if the seating area is used for study. (Care should be taken to avoid distracting reflections when direct down-light is used.) Aisle and exit lights, not visible to anyone seated, and shielded step-lights located on the side of the step, not the riser, should be provided for convenience and safety.

Stairways should be lighted so that the edges of all steps can be seen easily. Corridors should be lighted to provide an easy transition from daylight, which may be bright, to lower-level, classroom lighting. In locker areas light should be adequate to assure safety and to illuminate the interior of the locker. Lecture rooms should have comfortable general lighting, flexible enough for use at a lower level during film projection.

DWELLINGS

Until fairly recently most homes were lighted with a combination of pendant and surface-mounted fixtures, used with table and floor lamps. Many homeowners prefer the familiar lamp, which needs no actual installation. Lamps have been used since ancient times and probably will always be practical, but many other methods of residential lighting are available. Today many homes have no visible fixtures, and many practical systems are available that create special lighting effects.

Entrance areas should always be well lighted to avoid accidents and as a security measure. Small exterior fixtures can give a feeling of welcome

6–11 School lighting where the work is primarily of the head-down kind.

to guests, but they are not adequate for safety. Adjustable units under eaves or overhang, or where the fixture cannot be seen, can be directed onto sidewalks, shrubs, or trees, so that they provide interest and illumination without glare. Where glass walls or sliding glass doors are used, exterior lighting should complement interior lighting.

Halls require general lighting that is adequate for comfortable seeing, and special light for any mirrors. Stairways need enough direct, glare-free light so the riser can be readily distinguished from the tread.

6–12 Living- and family-room lighting that gives a sense of spaciousness. Cornice lighting illuminates the wall at right.

6–13 Mixed incandescent and fluorescent lighting in a dining room permits flexibility, as in the case (*right*) where candlelight is supplemented with only a single overhead light. Cove lighting is provided at the top edge of the draperies.

Living rooms and family rooms need good basic general lighting (Fig. 6–12) of a kind to make the space appear as large as possible (by having no dark areas) and also to make it all usable. Luminous ceilings with dimming controls, surface-mounted, recessed, or hanging fixtures, and cornice lighting—all are practical for these purposes, since all can be used to produce lighting that leaves no area dark. General lighting can also create a comfortable visual background so that lamps and other light sources do not contrast harshly with the background.

With the exception of fixtures that hang above a table, or wall brackets, the aim in lighting for dining is to provide illumination without seeing the source. For this purpose, built-in or recessed lighting is best. Cornice or valance lighting, recessed down-lights, or wall washers are effective. Panels of light behind fabric walls provide a soft, subtle illumination. In dining areas (Fig. 6–13) incandescent bulbs bring out the sparkle in china, silver, and glassware. Concealed fluorescent tubes can provide soft atmospheric lighting when candles are used. Fixtures suspended over a dining table, should be 30–36 inches above the table top—the higher the ceiling and the larger the fixture, the greater the distance from the table. Clear, low-wattage bulbs should be used in crystal chandeliers, frosted or coated bulbs in wood or metal ones. Other pendant fixtures over a table should provide upward as well as downward light. Such luminaires may be equipped so that the light can be used for studying, sewing, and so on. Special ceiling-mounted tracks allow for moving a luminaire horizontally.

6–14 Built-in (accident-proof) lighting in a child's bedroom (*top*) is supplemented with a table lamp in bedroom for adults (*below*).

Bedrooms

A child's bedroom, a teenager's, that of an elderly person, the master bedroom—all will have different lighting requirements (Fig. 6–14). Built-in lighting, which can be virtually accident-proof, is practical in a child's room, and it can supply both general and task lighting. Lighting in a bedroom has several functions. Soft, general lighting can be provided by valance or cornice lighting, surface ceiling fixtures and recessed downlights. For a desk, reading in bed, sewing, or putting on makeup, task lighting is needed. Various kinds of lamps are practical for the first three. Lamps flanking makeup mirrors should be approximately 36 inches apart, with translucent shades. The center of the shades should be the height of the face—about 15 inches above the dressing table for a seated position and 22 inches above a dresser for standing. Dimmer control is useful in bedrooms, especially those of babies and small children.

Kitchens

In a kitchen (Fig. 6–15), general lighting should provide diffuse overall illumination to reduce the contrast between task lighting and background. Fluorescent tubes are commonly used in kitchens because they are economical—supplying three

6–15 Moderate contrast between general and task lighting in a kitchen. Lighting over the work surfaces is an example of soffit lighting.

6–16   Lighting in a bathroom;
light adjacent to mirror falls
on user rather than mirror.

times the light of an incandescent for the same amount of electricity, they generate relatively little heat, their linear form is well suited to installation over counters and in soffits or valances, and certain of the fluorescent colors enhance the appearance of food. Incandescent bulbs, often used in ceiling fixtures, can cause distracting shadows unless placed to avoid them. There are special fixtures for every kind of work or storage area.

Bathrooms

Bathrooms (Fig. 6–16) need both general and task lighting. Mirrors should be well lighted, usually from above and both sides, which means that the light falls on the person, not the mirror; either fluorescent or incandescent bulbs can be used. Any bulb used in the bathroom, unless it is under twenty-five watts or coated, should have a translucent shield. Soft

White incandescent bulbs or Natural or Deluxe Warm White fluorescent tubes are flattering to complexion. Luminous ceilings are excellent for bathrooms.

In addition to the regular kinds of luminaires adapted for use in bathrooms, a number of special lamps are available—pedicare, heat, sun, and ozone (air-freshener).

BIBLIOGRAPHY

BIRREN, FABER. *Light, Color and Environment* (Reinhold, 1969). Biological and psychological aspects of color, indicating some of the possibilities for manipulation of environment through the use of light and color.

BIRREN, FABER, AND LOGAN, HENRY L. "The Agreeable Environment," *Progressive Architecture* (August 1960). Succinct summary of the use of light and color in making an "agreeable environment."

FLYNN, JOHN E., AND MILLS, SAMUEL M. *Architectural Lighting Graphics* (Reinhold, 1962). Technical information on how to use light and lighting design. Rigorous, but does not require technical training.

Illumination Engineering Society Handbook, 5th ed. (Waverly Press, 1972). Clear, well-organized handbook; virtually everything an interior designer need know about lighting.

KOHLER, WALTER. *Lighting in Architecture* (Reinhold, 1959). A classic (especially in the use of light as a design element); presents aspects of lighting for architects and aspects of architecture for lighting specialists.

LARSON, LESLIE. *Lighting and Its Design* (Whitney, 1964). An analysis of lighting problems and their solutions, including some outstanding ones. Photographs with comments, and a section illustrating design fixtures.

LOGAN, HENRY L. *Lighting Research, Its Impact—Now and Future* (Holophane, 1968). Helpful in keeping abreast of the many new applications of light.

7

7-1 A design in which floor
treatment is a major element.

FLOORS

AND FLOORCOVERINGS

Floors, functional as they are, can also be an important part of the total visual design. A floor can be fast, hard, smooth, and sleek, or slow, with a deep, soft carpet. Between the two extremes of a marble or a ceramic tile floor, for example, and one covered with a silky wool or fine synthetic carpet, there are many degrees. In selecting a floorcovering many practical questions need to be answered. These deal basically with the personal preferences of the client, the relation of the covering to other aspects of the design, and costs.

Installation and maintenance costs are extremely important in determining the selection of floorcovering. Wood, tile, resilient flooring, and carpeting are, of course, maintained in different ways, and maintenance methods used in schools, public buildings, stores, or shops—requiring special skills and equipment—are different from and more costly than those used in the home. Flooring is generally of three kinds: natural materials such as wood, brick, tile, stone, or concrete; resilient flooring, mainly vinyl, asbestos, asphalt, and other tile or sheet goods; and carpet. Because there is such a wide choice of color and design in both carpeting and resilient flooring, practical aspects should be considered first; color, pattern, and style second. These practical aspects include initial versus maintenance cost, durability, comfort relative to specific use, maintenance needed and available, ease of replacement of worn areas, and fire resistance, static electrical, acoustical, and safety characteristics. Several firms today that make both resilient and soft floorcoverings offer the same or coordinated patterns in both materials. After a decision has been made on performance, appearance is considered: color first, then pattern, if any, and suitability to the type of floor, the walls, and furnishings—the total design of the room. This requires answers to questions such as: Is the floor to be simply background, or is it of primary importance in the design (Fig. 7–1)? If the latter, how? Is a cool effect desired or a warm one? In what kind of room or space is it to be used? Lighting, both natural and artificial, should be considered as it affects the appearance of soft floor-covering more than of hard. If pattern is used, the scale must be consistent with any other pattern and with the size of the space. Rug size must be compatible with the area in which the rug is used. The wrong rug can throw a room completely out of balance.

Because of the great variety of carpeting available, it is imperative to get all information—usually from the dealer—on the performance that can be expected. Performance depends on the weight, type, and quality of yarn; the pile density (the number of tufts per square inch); and the pile height. In this evaluation the process used is also important. Pile density accounts for abrasion- and crush-resistance simply because the more tufts per square inch, the less wear on each. A deep pile will not make for quality carpet if pile density is not high.

The backing on a carpet is also important. Most tufted, knitted, and woven carpets have a latex backing that secures the surface yarns. Most good-quality carpets have a secondary backing (through which the yarn passes) laminated to this primary one. Jute is the natural material that has been used mainly for this backing; although it is still widely used, new synthetic backings—both woven and nonwoven—are also available. Which is best depends on the use to which the carpet will be put.

HARD FLOORING (NATURAL MATERIALS)

WOOD

Wood flooring was used in 950 B.C. in the temple of Solomon. Today the three most common kinds of wood floor design are strip flooring (long, narrow boards); random plank (composed of boards 3–12 inches wide); and parquet (Fig. 7–2), most costly and decorative. Parquet floors are made of short strips of wood laid in geometrical patterns, the most common of which are herringbone, checkerboard, basketweave, and *parquet de Versailles*, named after the palace where it is widely used.

Wood flooring has many advantages: it is relatively easily incorporated into a design, is comparatively easy to maintain, can be finished in many ways, and has a warmth, color range, and individual texture and grain that can contribute much to the character of a room.

7–2 Typical parquet patterns.

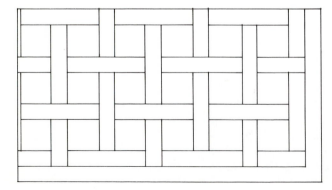

Traditionally used for flooring are oak, usually red or white; walnut, mainly from the United States; and pine, a softer wood. Less common are hard maple, which provides a sturdy, smooth floor (often used in gymnasiums), and teak, rosewood, and other rare woods, used for elegant but costly floors. Less traditional are relatively recently developed kinds that use different methods of installation and construction (mainly as plywood sheet), and are available in many finishes, colors, and woods. One of these, a laminated flooring, permits a beautiful surface at a cost lower than that of solid flooring. Block flooring, called "parquetry" in cases where it is made to simulate parquet, is also made in many contemporary designs. New finishes and new processes through which the wood is impregnated with plastics (see Chapter 10), have added greatly to the durability of wood flooring.

7–3 A marble floor, durable and "cool," in an elegant room.

STONE, CERAMIC, AND CONCRETE

Other natural materials used for floors in interiors are marble, slate, flagstone, brick, tile, and concrete (Fig. 7–3). Floors of these materials tend to be cold and uncomfortable for standing long periods.

Although color of the natural stones is limited, concrete can be painted. Concrete is very durable and can be used in precast form indoors. Marble, slate, and flagstone are durable, do not stain or spot easily, but can be hazardous in a bath or kitchen since they are slippery when wet. Terrazzo, small chips of marble

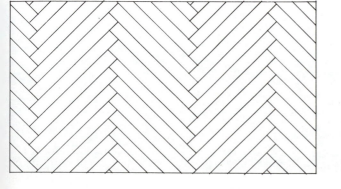

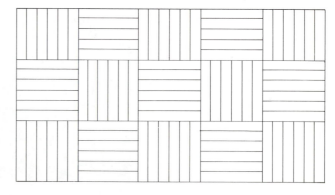

7–4   A tile floor that has been glazed with a sealer to prevent spotting.

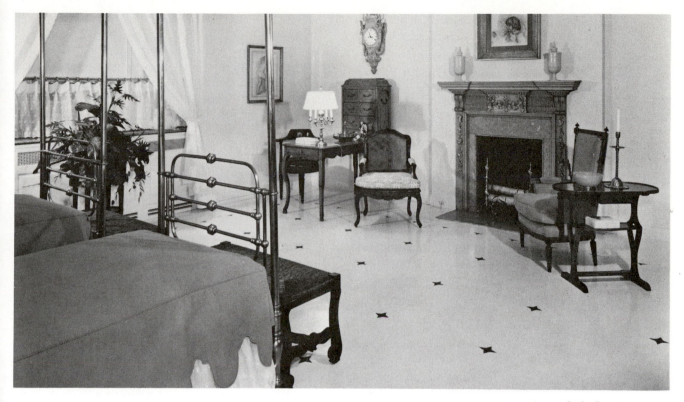

mixed with cement, the whole polished when set, makes a handsome and durable floor. Metal strips used in the expansion of terrazzo floors can be laid out in geometric patterns. Brick and tile (Fig. 7–4) will spot readily unless they are glazed or coated with a protective sealer. Clients should be given specific instruction on the care and maintenance of these materials.

RESILIENT FLOORCOVERINGS

Resilient floorcoverings, smooth-surface materials that spring back after indentation from pressure, offer good cushioning with a relatively hard and dense surface that is durable and may be finished so that the need for waxing and other maintenance is minimal. Methods of installation are simple. A variety of patterns, borders, inserts, and sizes of tile make it possible to create a custom design without custom-design cost. Some new vinyl floorings can be installed over existing floors and some are self-adhesive. The colors and patterns that are available range from the sharp and exciting to the soft and subtle.

The most common kinds of resilient flooring are vinyl-asbestos tile, asphalt tile, vinyl tile, sheet vinyl, and cushion-back sheet vinyl (Fig. 7–5). Others, used less frequently, are rubber and cork tile, felt-backed printed vinyl, and linoleum. Most resilient floorcoverings can be laid below grade, on grade, or suspended. Below grade means sunken partially or completely below the surrounding surface or ground and in direct contact with it or fill, which in turn rests on the ground. On grade is as the name indicates, again, on fill or in contact with the ground. The last method—suspended—refers to a covering laid above, on, or below grade level, but in all cases, with a minimum of 18 inches of well-ventilated space below the covering.

VINYL, ASPHALT, AND OTHER TILE

Vinyl-asbestos tile is one of the least expensive combinations of vinyl with another material, and is made in an assortment of colors and patterns suitable for almost any kind of interior. It has exceptional durability, is easily maintained, and resists deterioration by grease, oil, and mild acids. It can be used below grade, on grade, or suspended. It withstands moisture, abrasion, and great extremes of temperature, and is less noisy to the tread than asphalt tile.

Solid vinyl tile is pressed, polished tile that is used frequently in residential, institutional, and commercial installations. Exceptionally tough and high in tensile strength, it is not porous, and is smoother and therefore easier to maintain than most floor surfaces. It can be installed on or below grade if special adhesives are used. It is usually about ⅛ inch thick and is made in several standard sizes, as well as in special sizes and feature strips.

Asphalt tile is the least expensive of the resilient floorcoverings. Basically an all-purpose floor, it can be installed over both wood and masonry subfloors, below, on, or above grade. It is not greaseproof unless specially treated, is quite hard, and requires wax for proper maintenance.

Rubber tile is quiet and resilient.

Durable and easily maintained, it can be used below, on, or above grade.

Cork tile, available prefinished and in special sizes, is comfortable under foot, has only moderate resistance to grease and corrosive materials, and is made in three thicknesses. With a vinyl finish it is called "vinyl cork" or "custom cork." It can be installed on suspended floors only.

VINYL SHEET, LINOLEUM, AND PRINTED VINYL

Vinyl sheet, usually 6 feet wide, is durable enough to justify the expense of cementing it down for a long-term installation. It is made in a wide range of patterns with various backings and in several thicknesses. The heavier grades are generally specified for institutional and commercial areas. A cushion-backed form, comfortable to walk on and sound-absorbing, is more expensive.

Linoleum is easy to maintain and fairly durable. The first resilient flooring, it can be installed only over suspended concrete and certain suspended wood underfloors. It is still in use but is rapidly being replaced by other floorings.

Felt-backed printed vinyls are sold in standard rug sizes or by the yard. Many different patterns and colors are applied by the printing process, rotogravure. This flooring can be cemented in place, loose-laid, or modified loose-laid (cemented only at certain points) over suspended subfloors.

Special electrically conductive floors are used where static electricity is a hazard, as in hospital operating rooms where ignition of highly volatile materials (such as anesthetic gases) may cause explosions.

SOFT FLOORCOVERINGS

For many persons, carpets or rugs are the best floorcovering. Carpet of any kind provides a feeling entirely different from that of a hard-surface floor, whether the latter is wood, tile, or resilient flooring. Besides the obvious advantage of being softer to walk on and providing a feeling of luxury (without necessarily costing more), carpet minimizes or eliminates noise problems. The right combination of carpet and padding can absorb as much airborne noise (voices, music, appliances, and so on), as an acoustical ceiling. Floor surface noise (footsteps, the sound of dropped or dragged objects), can be prevented almost entirely by use of carpet. Impact noises that carry from a floor to the rooms below are also greatly reduced by carpet. With their qualities of quietness and softness, carpets suggest calmness, ease, and comfort. Carpeting is woven in widths from 27 inches to 18 feet; if seamless and more than 54 inches wide, carpet is called broadloom. (Rugs are distinguished from carpet in that they are finished on all sides and they are not usually fastened down.) Carpet is also available in easily installed, interchangeable squares or tiles that have an adhesive backing. The combination of kinds of fibers and methods of construction can be varied to produce carpet with characteristics specially suited to different uses—in homes, schools, institutions, and even out-of-doors.

FIBERS

The fibers most used in carpets today are wool, nylon, acrylic, modacrylic, polyester, polypropylene or olefin, Source (combination of nylon and polyester), and to a lesser degree, rayon and cotton. In 1965, for the first time, more broadloom was made of synthetic fibers than of wool, and the proportion has continued to increase. Wool, however, has truly passed the test of time, while the same cannot be said of any synthetics, with nylon possibly the only exception.

Wool

Wool is versatile in its acceptability and retention of dyes. It retains its appearance well, is resilient, and firm yet soft to walk on. Good wool carpets have a luxurious look, important to many interiors. They retain texture and do not mat, fuzz, or pill, the last a deficiency of some synthetics. They are rated high in resistance to soiling and fairly high in ease of stain removal, and are mildew- and flame-resistant. (A lighted match will char wool carpet, but the pile will cover the char area when brushed.) Many wool carpets are permanently moth-proofed (and will be so marked on their label) and can be processed to all but eliminate the tendency to build up static electricity charges. A new crimping process has made possible an improved fiber that has greater bulk and density, increased crush resistance, and a more luxurious look. The wide range of price in wool carpet reflects differences in quality of the yarn, method of construction, and cost of the design.

Nylon

Nylon was originally produced in small groups of short fibers called staples. Later, continuous-filament nylon, in which the fiber is drawn through without interruption, was developed. Nylon carpet is extremely durable, but in staple form, often used in blends of fibers, it may tend to fuzz or pill with wear. It has a high stain- and soil-resistance, and most spots are easily removed. It tends to accumulate static electricity charges but can be processed to minimize this; flame melts it (leaving a permanent spot), and it is moth- and mildew-proof, nonallergenic, and takes dye well. Some nylon (there are many kinds, made by different companies) shows an undesirable shininess. Tests show that soil-resistance of this carpet (made of "second-generation" nylon) is excellent and that its properties include a tendency to look fresh and new longer.

Acrylic

Acrylic carpets are the most like wool in appearance. Although they vary greatly in both appearance and performance, they are generally durable, resilient, resistant to soil, chemicals, and sunlight, and can be easily cleaned. They are relatively low in static electricity buildup. Flame melts the surface areas, just as it does nylon, leaving a scar or spot. (Some "acrylic" carpets are blended with modacrylic to increase their flame resistance.) Acrylic carpet takes and retains dye well.

Polypropylene (Olefin)

Polypropylene (olefin) carpet is resistant to soil and easily spot cleaned, has little tendency to accumulate static electricity, and is moth- and mildew-proof and nonallergenic. It is not as resilient as many other fibers and not as easily dyed. It is popular as indoor-outdoor carpeting.

Polyester and Source

Polyester carpet has a luxurious feel, good color retention, little static buildup, and is durable, resilient, stain- and soil-resistant, moth- and mildew-proof, and nonallergenic. Source, the first and only biconstituent (nylon and polyester), continuous-filament fiber, can be tailored to many needs in terms of performance qualities as well as appearance. Its silkiness is indirectly related to its durability. It is elegant, sturdy, moth- and mildew-proof and nonallergenic.

Cotton and Rayon

Cotton carpet is generally used today in small, washable rugs only. Rayon carpet takes dye especially well and is known for its fine range of colors. It is moth- and mildew-proof, but has little resiliency, and is not as durable as carpet made of other fibers.

PROCESSES

The quality of carpet depends not only on the fiber, but also on the way it is made. Most carpets today are either woven or tufted.

Weaving

The kinds of weaves are Wilton, Axminster, Brussels, velvet, and chenille. Wilton carpet, of various widths, is closely woven with a short, erect cut pile that gives it a fine texture. Worsted Wilton is made from long-fibered wool, which has great resilience; regular Wiltons are heavier, with a coarser pile. Brussels carpet, little used today, is the same as Wilton, except that the pile is uncut and the quality of the wool less consistent. The quality of the Axminster weave

depends on the number of tufts in each row; if there are fewer than five to the inch, it will not wear well. Velvet, the most frequently used form of woven carpet, is not very resilient and has a short pile. It can be made in a wide range of colors and, if made from good wool and closely woven, will wear well.

Loomed carpet is a form of woven carpet in which a low-loop fabric is bonded to a sponge-rubber cushion (Fig. 7–6). Such carpet is not thick, but wears well, the resilience depending entirely on the rubber base. It is laid like sheet goods, cemented to the floor, and is very difficult to remove.

7–6 Broadloom carpet gives warmth and quiet in an intimate room.

or backing (Fig. 7–7). In its machine-made form today, it can be made in any size, shape, color, and design, unlike woven rugs, which are limited in each of these aspects. Tufted carpet offers a variety of textures—determined by variations in the height of the pile and whether it is cut or uncut. A printing process called Colorset permits almost limitless color and design. Quality depends on that of the yarn and backing material, the density, thickness, and quality of the coating (usually a latex compound) applied. Custom-tufted carpet is designed for a particular area and is used for area rugs.

Knitting

Knitted carpet, like woven, is made in a single operation, although in the knitting process (unlike the case in weaving), the backing yarns are looped together, much as is done in hand knitting. It is inexpensive, can be made in any width, is used mainly for solids and tweeds, and the pile can be of different heights. If the carpet is close-knit, it wears well.

Needle Punch and Flocking

In the needle punch process, fibers (not yarn) are formed into a feltlike pad that is backed by latex, making a firm, dense, seamless construction. Originally made of polypropylene and used outdoors, on boat and sun decks, at poolside, and on terraces, it is now made (for indoor use) of polypropylene with wool, nylon, or acrylic fibers and is particularly useful for kitchens, bathrooms, family rooms, auditoriums, hospitals, and schools. It is inexpensive, and worn areas can be readily replaced or interchanged with

7–7   Bold design in a tufted rug.

Tufting

Most soft floorcovering installed in the United States today is tufted. Tufted carpet began as a handmade variation on the hooked rug, in which yarn is pulled through a burlap ground

parts from less used areas. It is not a luxury carpet.

Flocking creates a single-level, cut-pile, velvetlike surface. It has no resilience, is inexpensive, and is easily installed and maintained.

RUGS

CUSTOM AND HANDMADE

Many firms make handmade or partially handmade rugs (Fig. 7–8). Wool is the most popular fiber because it can produce an almost limitless variety of textures. Man-made fibers are being used, alone or in combination with wool. Handmade rugs are available in various combinations of sheared and unsheared, with a pile of one or more levels. The varieties of design, color, and shape are virtually unlimited, and the results are often such that the rugs are frequently hung as wall decoration. On the wall or the floor, their effect is strong, and they must be selected with care if they are to be unified with the rest of a design. Rugs designed and made by American Indians, in both traditional and modern designs, are sold through craft and other organizations. Also available are handhooked, braided, and woven rugs of cotton and wool made by individual craftsmen in the United States, Morocco, and many other countries.

SHAG

Most shag rugs are tufted. They have a pile with low density and random surface texture, in which yarns lie in all positions rather than the normal upright position of conventional

7–8 One of many possible designs in a handmade rug.

carpeting. Although the length of the pile varies, the tufts are always longer than in other carpets. Shag rugs are made of wool, nylon, acrylic, modacrylic, polyester, or polyvinylchloride fibers. They give a luxurious appearance at a moderate cost.

7–9 Oriental rugs confer
richness in any interior.

ORIENTAL

Oriental rugs are suitable for many kinds of interiors (Fig. 7–9). From both an esthetic and economic point of view they are among the finest floorcoverings made. Oriental rugs most frequently used today are Persian, Indian, Turkoman, Turkish, Caucasian, and Chinese.

Persian rugs are covered entirely with gracefully curved designs of conventionalized foliage—vines, leaves, and flowers—and some birds and ani-

mals; there is rarely a large center motif. Colors are soft and subtle.

Indian rugs also use foliage, flowers, and animals, but in designs that are not stylized, and seem taken almost directly from nature. The colors used are brighter and less subtle than those in Persian rugs.

Turkoman rugs are designed around geometric forms—primarily diamonds, octagons, stars, and squares. Dark red dominates, with browns and yellows also favored. These short-pile, close-weave rugs are often fringed.

Turkish rugs have designs that are more clearly defined than the others. Lines are straighter, leaves and flowers more pointed, and the general effect more angular. Colors are bright, with strong contrasts. An arched prayer niche as a center design is often used against a plain background.

Caucasian rugs were made in the region between the Caucasus and the Caspian Sea. The designs are crowded and resemble elaborate mosaics, with cartoonlike figures of people and animals. Caucasian rugs usually have wide borders and a variety of colors.

Some fine Oriental rugs are still being made, but few relative to the production in earlier times. Before the beginning of the nineteenth century, rug-making was often a family affair, and designs were passed on from father to son. With the development of interest in these rugs in the Western world and of means for transporting them here, the demand grew. With increased production, materials, dyes, and workmanship have suffered somewhat.

7–10 An Aubusson rug with typical center medallion and floral motif.

AUBUSSON AND SAVONNERIE

From France come the Aubussons, Savonneries, and many of the needle-point rugs. The Aubussons are woven like tapestries (sometimes by machine), but are more coarse and heavier than the tapestries (Fig. 7–10).

Today's designs often reproduce those popular in the seventeenth and eighteenth centuries—during the reigns of Louis XV and Louis XVI and the Directoire and Empire periods. There are usually center medallion, floral motif, scroll, and arabesques; the colors are soft and subtle. Aubussons and Savonneries are also made in modern designs. The latter are hand-knotted, made with a cut pile and a much deeper weave than the Aubussons, and look richer.

CUSHIONS AND PADS

Carpet cushions or pads are important to the wearability, comfort, and appearance of any soft floorcovering. Several types are available: felted, made of hair or a combination of hair and jute; flat or rippled sponge rubber; and polyurethane. All types are made in various weights and thicknesses. The cushion should be chosen in relation to the carpet; a skimpy carpet will not be made to seem more generous by a thick cushion, and a flimsy cushion will be recognizable even under a thick carpet. The right combination of pad and carpet will produce either a very resilient feeling when walked on, a very firm one, or something between the two, whichever is desired. In general, hair- and jute-felted cushions work well under rugs or carpets that have a tendency to stretch or ripple. It is wise to use a firm cushion under stair carpeting. Much of the new carpet intended for use in kitchens, recreation or family rooms, baths, and public buildings has a foam-rubber backing. Heavy sponge rubber is better for use in living rooms and bedrooms. Inexpensive pads made from scrap material shortens the life of a carpet.

OTHER ASPECTS

To deal with the static electricity charges that accumulate when a person walks across a carpet (particularly wool or nylon carpet), a process has been developed in which tiny hairlike pieces of metal are blended with the carpet fibers. (The process has also been found to increase soil resistance.) Antistatic-charge sprays, powders, and liquids are available for treating carpets and rugs that have not been processed with metal. These chemical treatments, however, are not permanent, and some may even cause carpet to soil more readily.

Installation is very important to the way a carpet wears. Usually a good dealer provides good installation. Faulty installation can reduce the life of carpet.

BIBLIOGRAPHY *

CON, J. M. *Carpets from the Orient* (Universe, 1966). Basic information on types of oriental carpets and where they are made. Brief and easy to understand.

KENT, WILLIAM WINTHROP. *Rare Hooked Rugs* (Pond-Ekberg, 1941). Collection of handsome hooked rugs organized by type of design.

LIEBTRAU, PREBEN. *Oriental Rugs in Color* (Macmillan, 1962). Well organized, basic and brief, with fine illustrations.

* New floorcovering materials are appearing so rapidly that those seeking the most up-to-date information should investigate such periodicals as *Interiors, Interior Design, Architectural Forum, Architectural Record,* and *Progressive Architecture.* Material is also available from The Carpet and Rug Institute, Dalton, Ga. 30720; The Wool Bureau, Inc., New York, N.Y. 10017; and Asphalt and Vinyl Asbestos Tile Institute, New York, N.Y. 10017.

8

Walls define and enclose, determine and help shape the character of interior space; they provide privacy, absorb or reflect light and sound, and insulate against cold, heat, and noise.

Since walls are large in area and in terms of investment, their treatment is of major importance. During the planning process (Chapter 4), the first thing to decide concerning a wall and its surface is the specific function of each: Does the wall simply separate two areas, or is sound absorption involved as well? How much privacy must the wall provide? How should light and heat be affected by the wall? Is the wall treatment featured in the design scheme, or will it function mainly as background?

WALL MATERIALS AND FINISHES

Interior walls may be of plaster, wood, brick, stone, concrete, glass, metal, or plastic. (Plastics can be had in sheet as well as tile form.)

Plaster walls are usually finished with paint or some kind of wallcover-ing. Wood walls, too, are often painted, or covered, but may also be stained, or finished with a clear coating. Wood walls may be paneled, and wood and plaster are often combined.

Architectural features that are made of wood (old or in reproduction)—for example, a cornice and baseboard, and perhaps a dado and paneling—can be finished in several ways. The wood can be painted one color, and the wall (where of plaster) a different color, thus emphasizing the architecture. Again, if there is wood paneling, the architecture can be featured by using two colors, or by picking out the important moldings in a color of slightly different value from that on the wall. Stained wood can be protected with a finish that provides any surface, from matte to gloss, and is easily maintained. In to-day's interiors, plywood is the most commonly used wood. It is available in countless woods and finishes—most of which are exceptionally resistant to scratching and marring—that can be safely cleaned with a damp cloth and are guaranteed for the life of the building. The properties that

WALLS, WALLCOVERINGS,

AND ARCHITECTURAL ELEMENTS

relate to the performance of a wood are specific gravity, supporting strength, stiffness, hardness, shock resistance, and potential shrinkage. Data concerning these qualities are readily available from dealer or manufacturer.

Brick or stone—substantial, easy to maintain, and fireproof—can be waterproofed or given a clear, dust-resistant finish. They should be specially selected for interior use as to color, size, and texture, and it should be kept in mind that they reflect sound more than most interior-wall materials.

Concrete, in blocks or as a continuous poured surface, is used with and without paint and is less expensive than brick or stone. Mixed with exposed stone aggregate, it provides another interesting surface.

Metal is often used for movable walls with good sound-damping properties. Clay, ceramic, rubber, cork, or vinyl tile can be applied to almost any kind of wall. Ceramic tile can be glazed or unglazed and is available in a variety of colors that can be combined in a pattern. Unglazed tile, quarry tile, and ceramic mosaic are sold attached to paper sheets for easy installation. Glazed tile is available in matte or glossy finish and in a variety of sizes, patterns, and shapes. Sheets are usually 2 x 6 or 2 x 10 inches, but can be ordered in special sizes. Porcelain enamel tiles are also available with a covering of leather or aluminum. All are easily cleaned and very durable.

Vinyl wall tile also comes in a wide range of colors, textures, and patterns. Certain kinds will conceal minor bulges or cracks in a wall.

Cork tile lasts longer when treated with a stain- and moisture-resistant preparation.

Free-standing screen walls or partitions are made of wood (sometimes in combination with cabinets and shelves), in filigree, of fiberglass or plastic, and of wood-framed paper (shoji screens—light, translucent panels, some of which slide).

Some fabrics are made especially so that they can be stretched and pasted or tacked to walls. Others are laminated to a backing for easier installation and longer use. Felts improved for use on walls will not shrink and have been made soil- and flame-resistant, and are available in a wide range of light-fast colors.

PAINT

Paint is the least expensive and easiest to apply material for use on walls, and can be mixed to match other surfaces. Paints are of three kinds—flat, semigloss, and gloss. The degree of washability depends on the quality and kind of paint: flat paints usually will not be washable, but gloss, semigloss, and dull enamels have a hard enough surface to withstand modern cleaning products. Gloss paint reflects the most light. (In testing colors on walls, use large samples—painted on pieces of cardboard or wood at least 2 x 2 feet—and try each on a window wall, the opposite wall, and a side wall. Let samples dry completely before making any judgments, and check them in every light including whatever artificial light will be used.)

Methods in manufacturing wall-coverings have advanced rapidly in the past three decades. Light-fast colors were first used in 1928, and washable colors at popular prices became available in 1934. Silkscreening began to replace wood-block prints in the forties, and many scrubbable, prepasted, and pretrimmed papers were introduced in the fifties. Today there are sheet plastics that are almost indestructible and chemically treated so that they can be removed from the wall without prior soaking with water.

WALLPAPER AND OTHER SHEET COVERINGS

Many kinds of wallcoverings are used today: special paper, paper sized with a protein plastic, hence washable (but stainable by certain liquids); pa-

8–1 Some wallcovering patterns; *left to right:* textured, floral, and geometric, and (*below*) damask.

per with a thick plastic coating that is stain-resistant and easily washed; vinyl laminated to paper; paper laminated to lightweight woven cloth (natural or synthetic) and with or without vinyl coating; vinyl laminated to lightweight nonwoven cloth (natural or synthetic); vinyl laminated to paper or nonwoven fabric; natural materials impregnated with vinyl; flocked paper or cloth, which simulates damask or cut velvet; foil on a paper or fabric back (printed or plain); embossed papers or plastics (with or without ink); and carpeting, especially the flocked variety.

Patterns in wallcoverings are of several kinds (Fig. 8–1): *textured*

8–2   Wallcovering (carried onto
the ceiling) helps soften the
visual impact of an awkward
corner.

patterns which offer actual or simulated surfaces of many materials, particularly fabrics and wood; *geometric patterns*, in which, because a large area is being covered, care must be taken (especially in the case of op-art patterns) to stimulate but not tire or irritate the eye; *floral patterns*, the most frequently used, and available in a great variety of representations, from realistic to abstract; *damask patterns*, a kind of stylization of natural forms; *toiles*, formal and traditional, small landscape-with-figure patterns in one color and often made with a matching fabric. Wallcoverings are also made in *scenics* and *trompe l'oeil* which are not, strictly speaking, pattern. Trompe l'oeil, a method of representation that aims to create an illusion of three-dimensionality, is rarely used in a repeat design. Scenics may be repeated but not in the manner of a conventional repeat pattern.

In addition to their mood and decorative functions, wallcoverings can help to correct architectural defects (Fig. 8–2). A pattern with strong vertical elements, for example, will make a ceiling seem higher, and a horizontal pattern will produce the opposite effect. A small-scale, light-colored pattern can make a room appear larger. (Light colors generally give a feeling of greater space; stronger ones the opposite.) Pattern used on walls should be harmonious with the color, scale, and general feeling of any other patterns in a room. A matching wallcovering and fabric can be used effectively in a room.

Each kind of wallcovering requires its own kind of maintenance procedures. The manufacturer will supply such information, which should be passed on to the client.

WALL ELEMENTS

Architectural elements—windows, doors, chimney pieces, and such finishing touches as baseboards and cornices—are planned and used in relation to the walls.

WINDOWS

Windows have three general purposes—to admit, shape, and direct light; to permit ventilation; and to frame a view. Many different kinds of windows are available (Fig. 8–3). Well-made windows will reduce heat loss or summer heat gain by 15 to 35 percent, are easy to operate, and require minimal maintenance. Wood-frame windows have superior insulating value, especially when equipped with weather stripping—of vinyl, stainless-steel, or wool pile. The better aluminum-frame windows are anodized or have a baked-enamel finish. Steel-frame windows, although specially treated, must be painted periodically.

Although climate, prevailing winds, and exposure to sun are considerations in locating windows, individual requirements of space and function are primary; for example, in a bedroom, privacy, ventilation, and the location of the beds are important in determining the type of window to be used and its placement. A kitchen window should provide good ventilation, as much natural light as is available, and when possible, a view. In other buildings—offices, factories, schools, hospitals—windows serve different purposes in different areas, and height and placement might be determined, for example, by whether they are used by persons who are seated or in bed, or by people who are standing.

Windows are fixed or movable. In air-conditioned buildings, it is usually unnecessary for windows to be movable, although there are indications that people prefer windows that can be opened. There are five basic kinds of movable windows: double-hung, casement, sliding, awning, hopper.

A double-hung window, the most widely used, has two halves (sashes); the sash that is the lower when in the normal, closed position can be moved up or down in channels in front of the upper sash, which in turn slides up or down in channels behind the lower. A double-hung window is available that has a pivoting sash (or one that can be lifted out) so that the window exterior can be washed from the inside.

Casement windows are hinged at the side and usually swing out. They permit a complete opening of the window space (rather than only half the space, as in the double-hung window), but clearance must be allowed for anyone passing on the outside. Casement windows are, therefore, screened on the inside. In those that open out, the crank that operates the window does so through the screen, from the inside. Some screens are available that operate on a roller, like a window shade.

Bay or bow windows can be double-hung or casement type. Often the center section is fixed and the sides movable.

Sliding windows operate like a double-hung window on its side,

8–3 Five kinds of windows; *left to right:* double-hung, casement, sliding, awning, and hopper.

moving horizontally on a track at head and sill. One or both panes may be movable. Sliding windows are easier to reach and handle than a double-hung window and allow the same amount of opening (half the window).

The awning window is hinged at the top so that it swings outward from the bottom. Unless used in a basement, one is usually placed below a fixed window, or several are stacked one above the other. A version of this latter type is called a jalousie, which is composed of a number of side-mounted strips of glass, each about three inches wide, whose angle is adjustable in much the same way as the slats of a Venetian blind. This feature permits air in while keeping rain

out. Jalousies are not, however, adequate for severe winter weather since the strips do not fit tightly together when closed.

A hopper window is hinged at the bottom and swings *in* from the top like an inverted awning window. It is less effective in controlling drafts but useful where no other window can be placed, often below a large, fixed picture window.

Clerestory windows, usually fixed, are windows placed high in a wall, usually above an adjacent, lower roof. Skylights, practical in both residential and commercial interiors, are usually fixed.

For windows made today that require traditionally small panes—oblong, square, or diamond-shaped—

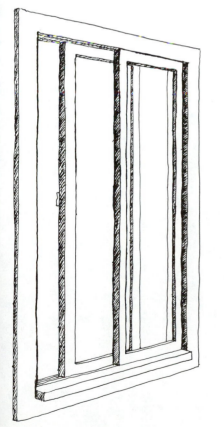

8–4 Some shades and blinds: matchstick (*opposite*), roller (*above left*), and vertical strip.

muntin bars are available, which simulate such panes, but can be snapped out for cleaning.

Shades and Blinds

Daylight is desirable in most interior spaces if it can be properly controlled—a task often performed by shades and blinds (Fig. 8–4). Roller shades, the most commonly used means of controlling natural light and the simplest, are available in a wide range of colors and textures, with or without design. They may be vinyl-coated for long wear and easy maintenance, as well as flame-resistant or flame-proof and soil-resistant. They are also made of highly translucent materials for light without glare, or opaque, for complete room darkening.

Shades act as a barrier to outside noises and reduce heat loss in cold weather. Blackout shades are also made in a wide range of colors, in sheen or in matte finish. Fabrics are laminated to regular shades, and shade cloth can also be used as wallcovering. Installation may be regular roller or reversed roller (roller on the back), roller mounted top or bottom, or up and down (one shade operating from the top, another from the bottom). Shades are available for special installations—such as around air conditioners, for windows in a slanted roof, or for skylights.

Venetian blinds are flexible in application and effective in controlling light. Their slats can be angled readily to let in light from above or below, without sacrificing privacy, and they can be completely opened or closed. Adjustment is by cord or plastic rod. Venetian-blind slats can be made of wood, but are more commonly of light metals. They can be any color available in paint, one color inside and another outside, color on one side and pattern on the other, or laminated with a fabric. A type with one-inch slats and almost invisible tapes is used in many dwellings and office and public buildings.

Vertical blinds, made of strips 3½– 7 inches in width, are made of plain cotton or with vinyl backing and are available with a single track at the top or with track at both top and bottom. They are flexible, can be turned to either side at any angle, and can be set so that they cover a window completely or almost not at all. They are made in plain colors or patterned, usually on the inside. Metal blinds, similar in appearance to Venetian blinds, but installed with slats vertical, are used commercially.

Other means of controlling light: shutters (inside or outside the window), pulley-adjusted blinds (such as matchstick type), awnings, and long, vertically suspended strands of beads. The last have little flexibility in application.

Curtains

While decorative window shades and various kinds of blinds are often used without curtains, in most homes, hotels, motels, and private clubs, curtains will add interest and warmth. They may be featured in the design scheme or used functionally as background, and can also help to regulate light and increase privacy (Fig. 8–5). Curtains can have acoustical value, alter the apparent size or proportion of windows and height of ceilings, and conceal certain architectural defects. A curtain has a function—to shut off, cover, conceal, or decorate a space or object—and may be made so that it can be drawn across, back, or up.

Sheer curtains are hung either inside or outside the window frame. Used alone—that is, without other curtains at the sides—they look better hung from the frame or the wall. For proper hanging, the curtain needs 100 percent fullness (achieved by using twice the cloth needed to cover the opening) and a double, weighted hem. Sheer curtains that hang over the glass—"glass" or "casement" curtains—are rarely pulled back. Curtains on casement windows that open in must be hung directly on the casement so that they move with the window.

8–5 Curtains: "tie-back" (*opposite*), straight, and (*below*) a heavy, fixed type with cornice.

Slightly heavier but unlined curtains filter the light and provide some privacy. Heavier curtains, lined or unlined, may hang alone or over the sheer curtains.

Unlined curtains of medium weight are often made of fabrics that have a variety of weaves, textures, and patterns not found in sheer fabrics. They can provide more interest than sheer curtains but appear lighter and airier than lined ones. They are made to draw or remain stationary. When selecting an unlined curtain, one must consider how it will look from outside by day (when daylight will make the pattern), in effect, part of the exterior.

Heavy curtains can be had in the greatest variety of styles and fabrics. They can be fixed, or made so they can be drawn (either by hand or motor), or be fastened back by means of a "tie-back." Cornices and valances with varying amounts of decorative trim are often used over these curtains.

For lined curtains, special fabrics, which have good insulating qualities, are commonly used. Very heavy curtains may have a second lining, often of cotton flannel, for added light control and improved hanging. The heading is the portion of the curtain that stands above the rod. The most common headings are: the French heading, box pleats, and cartridge pleats. The hooks or rings that hold a curtain up are fastened to the back of the bottom of the heading. Simpler to take down and easier to use types of curtain installation have plastic carriers sewn into the top hem of a permanently pleated fabric and attached to a special tape. These systems have several advantages besides ease of operation and of removal: folds remain vertical, and, in general, the curtains hang better, take up much less space when open, are simpler to clean, and operate more easily and smoothly.

DOORS

Doors have decreased somewhat in importance with the growing popularity of open-plan interiors. But privacy, still a necessity in many situations, requires doors. They are also essential for safety, as sound barriers, and to shut out weather. Many doors are made of materials other than the traditional wood; metal, glass, and plastics are common door materials (Fig. 8–6).

Most doors are hinged or are of the sliding, folding, or revolving type (with or without a latch or lock). Double-hinged doors swing both ways and are useful where it is important that a door open away from the user—for example, in the case of a waiter passing between kitchen and dining areas with laden trays. Self-closing doors offer safety and privacy and reduce heat loss. In the past, simple or elaborately carved doors of wood were used, and each period had its own style of panels and special moldings. Few such doors are made today; most hinged doors are of plywood or metal sheath over a light core with a plain trim. Hardware is also usually simple, generally polished steel, aluminum, or chrome, although more elaborate hardware of brass, bronze, or steel is also available.

Entrance doors of plate glass, often specially tempered and sometimes in a metal frame, may swing one or both ways. Some aluminum doors have louvers that operate in a way similar to those of a jalousie window; they can be adjusted to let in air and keep out rain and wind, and also permit

8–6 Doors: wood panel (*above*) in a classic English Georgian room, Victorian glass and wood (*far left*), and flush door of plywood.

a person to see and talk to anyone outside without opening the door.

Sliding exterior doors of double layers of glass, properly installed, have excellent thermal insulating properties. They are usually installed in pairs and slide one behind the other, and not into the wall. Interior doors may also slide into a kind of pocket installed in the wall, which thus allows the doorway to be completely open. Heavy sliding doors have tracks both at the top and on the floor; lighter ones may be suspended from a ceiling track only. They are made of wood, metal, glass, or a combination that may include plastic.

Folding doors are good where it is necessary to save space, and they can be used as room dividers. They are made of wood (in many finishes), plastic (both rigid and soft), and metal, and have a ceiling track and (in the heavier ones and those with acoustical properties) a floor track. Folding doors can provide great flexibility in schools and institutions.

FIREPLACES

Today, free-standing fireplaces are available, but most are still built as part of a wall. A fireplace is often the functional or design focal point of a room. Although not reliable for heating, it can provide enough heat for comfort in a limited area in relatively mild weather. An appropriate design for a fireplace and/or its mantel can range from a delicate, carved chimney piece of the Louis XVI period to a simple opening in a heavy stone or brick wall (Fig. 8–7). An opening can be just that in a plain wall, or it can be surrounded by a molding. There are many kinds of fireplace furnishings—grates, andirons, tools, and fenders, modern as well as traditional.

8–7 Fireplaces: (*left to right*) Louis XV marble; fieldstone in a country house; and free-standing, sheet metal; (*at left, below*) plaster in Spanish style.

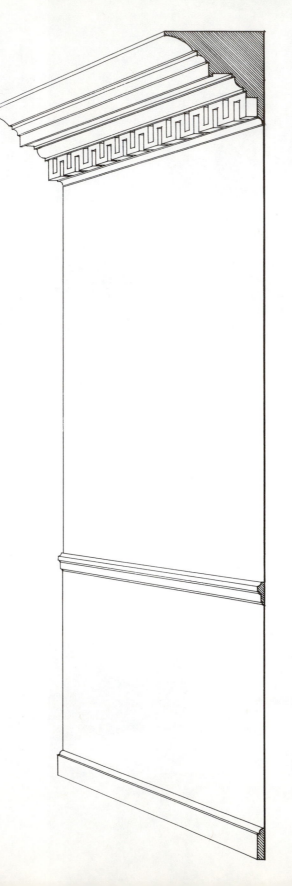

8–8 *From top to bottom, typical traditional cornice, dado, and baseboard.*

The free-standing fireplace has the advantage of flexibility and low construction cost. There are a number of kinds available, with a variety of chimneys and vents and a corresponding range in price. They can be metal (black or in color) or pottery. Most burn wood or can be adapted for use with gas or electricity, and have a protective screen across the opening. Information important to the installation of such a fireplace is the gauge of the sheet metal of which it is made, the type of floor protection required, whether the vent pipes can be used with an existing chimney, the type of vent, and the fuel for which it is designed.

CORNICE, BASEBOARD, AND DADO

A cornice (Fig. 8–8) was traditionally the crowning member of an architectural composition, the decorative element that provided the transition from wall to ceiling. The term now usually refers to the horizontal molding along the top of a wall. In contemporary building, the wall elements may simply meet, without the intervention of any clear-cut member like a cornice.

A baseboard provides transition from floor to wall, and today is usually quite simple. Dados, rarely found in today's architecture, constitute the lower part of a wall when it is separated from the area above by a molding. It may be a different material or color.

BIBLIOGRAPHY

ACKERMAN, PHYLLIS. *Wallpaper, Its History, Design and Use* (Tudor, 1923). Useful, but rather prescriptive.

BARROWS, CLAIRE M. *Living Walls,* ed. and with an introduction by William Justema (Wallcoverings Council, 1968). Up-to-date information on wallcoverings.

ENTWISTLE, E. A. *The Book of Wallpaper; A History and an Appreciation* (Barker, 1954). An interesting history of the development of wallpapers. Does not deal with nonpaper coverings.

MC CLELLAND, NANCY V. *Historic Wallpapers from Their Inception to the Introduction of Machinery* (Lippincott, 1924). Easy-to-read, impeccable sourcebook of the history of wallpaper. Presently out of print.

9

Although the words "fabrics" and "textiles" are frequently used interchangeably, they are not synonymous. Fabric is any kind of cloth and may be woven, knit, felted, or tufted; textiles are only those fabrics produced by a process of weaving that interlaces two systems of yarn (of natural or synthetic fibers) at right angles to each other. Lengthwise threads are the *warp*, and the crosswise, the *weft* or *filling*. Knit fabrics are made of one or more yarns lying in the same direction and interlaced by loops. Felted fabrics are made from wool, fur, or hair, cut into short fibers that are matted together by pressure, chemical action, moisture, or heat. A tufted fabric is made by inserting extra yarn into the openings of an existing ground fabric. Except in carpets, tufted fabrics are rarely used in interiors.

Textiles constitute the major portion of fabrics used in interior environment, although the use of knit, felted, or laminated fabrics is increasing. In the past, few interiors could be completed without the use of textiles—for floorcoverings, in furniture, on walls, and for curtains. Today it is possible to dispense with fabrics in an interior by using vinyls or other plastics. However practical and functional such an interior would be, fabrics remain one of the most important components in furnishing an interior and offer a vast palette of design, color, and function. Fibers, the basic strands from which yarns are spun, are of two basic kinds—natural and man-made. Natural fibers are derived from animals and plants. Cotton and flax, and to a much lesser degree, hemp and jute, are the most common plant fibers; mohair, silk, and wool are the basic animal fibers. Man-made fibers used in interiors include those made from cellulose, chemicals taken from other substances, and chemicals having a mineral base.

NATURAL FIBERS

FROM PLANTS

Cotton

The cotton fiber ("staple") varies in length up to two inches ("long staple"). The United States produces

FABRICS

more cotton than any other country, but most of the finest, long-staple cotton comes from Egypt.

Still used widely despite the rapid rise in popularity of synthetics, cotton rates high in versatility, economy, and durability (Fig. 9–1). It takes dyes that are fast to laundering and sunlight, is static free, and can be made stain- and water-repellent, weather- and wrinkle-resistant, and waterproof. It can be laminated or bonded to other fabrics as a backing.

Many different kinds of fabrics, light or heavy, delicate or strong, are made from it in a variety of styles and qualities—the finest and most luxurious as well as the toughest and most durable. Blended with other fibers it contributes its good qualities to a number of textiles.

Flax

From the stem of the flax plant come the fibers—sometimes as long as two feet—of which linen is made. More expensive than cotton, linen has most of cotton's good qualities, plus a few of its own. It is suitable for upholstery (Fig. 9–2), slipcovers, both

heavy and sheer curtains, and as a wallcovering. It is absorbent, which helps make it sound-deadening, is mothproof, and resistant to mildew, bacteria, and dust. It can be made wrinkle-resistant. The high tensile strength of linen yarns has made pos-

9–1 Cotton fabrics enliven a room in a maternity hospital.

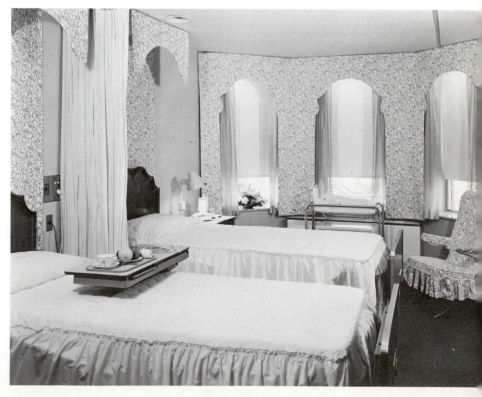

9–2 The durability of linen put to use in chair and sofa upholstery.

sible a variety of weaves, ranging from lacy to heavy textures. Neither direct sunlight nor artificial heat affects its dimensional stability or color. Sheer, open-weave casements of linen control sun excellently while permitting light and air to come through. Solid vat-dyed colors in linen will not fade in the sun. Linen can also be blended with cotton, rayon, mohair, and other fibers for reasons of economy or esthetic effect.

Jute and Hemp

Fabrics made from jute resemble linen but are much coarser and less resilient. Jute was once used mainly for furniture webbing, carpet backing, and burlap bags. It is still widely used for backing and in burlap that is softer than bagging and comes in many colors useful for curtains, wallcoverings, and smaller items, such as cushions and table mats. Hemp is stiff and coarse and can be made only into heavy, rough fabrics; it is used primarily in carpets and rugs.

FROM ANIMALS

Silk

Silk, long considered the finest fiber, was probably developed in China at least two centuries before the birth of Christ. Its source (the silkworm's spun cocoon) and the way it was made were such well-kept secrets that silk was not made in Europe until the ninth century. The fiber is fine, lustrous, and very long—sometimes several hundred yards. It is the strongest of the natural fibers and its smoothness reduces the problem of abrasion. A protein fiber, silk is wrinkle- and mildew-resistant, moth-proof, and takes dye well. It is practical in many different weaves and textures for curtains (Fig. 9–3), upholstery, and wallcoverings.

Wool

Wool was probably known and used before any other fiber. Wool fibers come from the fleece of sheep, goats, llamas, and alpacas. Mohair, classed as a separate fiber by some manufacturers, comes from the Angora goat. It is often blended with wool, to which it adds resilience and body. The length of the wool fiber varies considerably. Wool is often blended with cotton, rayon, and/or nylon. It tends to soil readily, but can be treated to increase soil resistance. Some wools are processed to reduce shrinkage.

SYNTHETIC FIBERS

Synthetic fibers [1] are made by a process similar to that used by the silkworm, in which a liquid is extruded that solidifies into a continuous filament when it comes in contact with the air. In the three principal variations in the manufacture of synthetics, a solution is forced through tiny holes into either warm or cool air, or into a chemical bath, where it solidifies. (A list of the trade and generic names of synthetic fibers is provided in the Appendix.)

1. A *Man-Made Fiber Fact Book* is available free from The Man-Made Fiber Producers Association, Inc., 350 Fifth Avenue, New York, N.Y. 10001.

9–3 Silk curtains contribute richness.

CHEMICALLY TREATED CELLULOSE

Rayon

Originally (in the nineteenth century) intended as a substitute for silk, rayon, which is primarily a cellulose product, now stands on its own as a beautiful and useful fabric.

Although marketed under forty-five different trade names, there are four basic kinds: viscose, cuprammonium, high wet-modulus, and saponified.

Viscose rayon is about half as strong as silk, weaker than cotton and linen, but stronger than wool. Despite its weaknesses, it can be made into fairly durable, economical fabrics. It wrinkles more readily than most cellulosic fibers but its crease-resistance can be enhanced. It hangs well, absorbs dyes easily, and has a high resistance to deterioration by sunlight. It washes well, but with repeated washings may shrink.

Cuprammonium rayon is about as strong as regular viscose rayon (both lose up to 70 percent of their strength when wet). Cuprammonium rayon can be made in different textures. It is especially suitable for curtains because it hangs well. It takes dyes easily and prints well, but may fade over a long period. It is made in sheer fabrics as well as heavier-weight cloth. Cuprammonium rayon is moth-resistant, but will mildew if damp for long.

High wet-modulus rayon [2] is almost as strong as cotton and retains its strength when wet. Three fabrics are made of this product, each with its own special qualities: Zantrel, which is in the price range of combed cotton and is just as strong, is less abrasion-resistant than cotton and will mildew. It is somewhat wrinkle-resistant, hangs gracefully, takes a wide range of dyes, and is moth-resistant. It can be treated to reduce shrinkage to 1 percent, and can be blended with cotton, triacetate, nylon, polyester, and acrylic fibers (see

below). Lirelle, a little less wrinkle-resistant than Zantrel, is more absorbent, and has been successfully blended with cotton. Avril, which has qualities similar to those of Zantrel, but is less elastic, is fairly wrinkle-proof, more absorbent, does not sag, and can be effectively blended with cotton.

Saponified rayon is sold only under the trade name Fortisan.[3] It has been used for parachutes and in other military applications and is very strong—three times as strong as silk. It is frequently combined with other fibers (as the warp) for its strength and to produce a shimmering surface. It does not sag, has excellent draping qualities, and tends to shed dirt. It must be dry-cleaned, as it will shrink if washed, and it is more difficult to dye than the other rayons. It is moth-resistant but will mildew.

Acetate

Acetate differs from rayons in that it is composed of compounds in addition to those derived from cellulose. Acetate yarns are produced by many different companies under different trademarks. The fibers are made into two kinds of yarn—continuous filament and spun; the character of the fabric depends on which of these yarns is used, as well as on the construction and finish. Acetate rayon is weaker than other rayons, but more wrinkle-resistant. It is resistant to deterioration by light, and unlike other cellulose fibers, is highly resistant to mildew. It is made in both sheer and heavy fabrics and hangs very well, but is difficult to dye. It is often blended with other fibers—mainly wool and nonacetate rayon—to reduce its cost.

2. Zantrel, Lirelle, and Avril, trade names used in this section, designate products of American Enka Company, Courtoulds North American, Inc., and American Viscose Company, respectively.

3. Celanese Corporation, New York, N.Y.

NONCELLULOSE FIBERS

Nylon

Nylon is a textile name that designates a group of chemical compounds classified as polyamides. Because nylon fibers can be produced with such a wide variety of characteristics they can be fabricated so as to simulate the appearance of other fabrics. Nylon is very strong and has high resistance to abrasion. Its strength is not lost with age. It is wrinkle- and dirt-resistant and hangs extremely well (Fig. 9–4). Resistant to deterioration by light, it is mothproof and will not mildew, is fairly easy to dye, and resists fading. It can be treated so that accumulations of static electricity, which make the fabric cling, can be prevented. It can be blended with cotton, wool, silk, and rayon.

Polyester

Polyester is produced from elements derived from coal, air, water, and petroleum. Fabrics made of it are wrinkle-resistant, easy to care for, washable, quick-drying, and have good resistance to deterioration by sunlight. They are not affected by moths or mildew, have excellent dimensional stability, and take dye well. Polyester fabrics may be smooth or nubby, compact or open. The fibers can be blended with cotton, wool, rayon, and nylon.

Acrylic

Used extensively for carpets and rugs and popular for upholstery and curtains, acrylic-fiber fabrics are fairly strong, luxurious to the touch, and lightweight, mothproof, and soil- and wrinkle-resistant. When mildew forms on an acrylic, it has no effect

9–4 Nylon mesh fabric and carpet in an interior that departs sharply from conventional 90-degree angularity.

9–5 Glass fiber curtains transmit light while preserving privacy.

on the fabric and can simply be wiped off. Specially developed dyes provide a wide range of colors resistant to fading by sunlight. Acrylics are fabricated in light or heavy fibers. The light ones are soft and luxurious; the heavy have the feel and bulk of wool. They can be blended with cotton, wool, rayon, acetate, and nylon.

Modacrylics

Modacrylics are increasing in importance because of their ability to resist flame—a quality that is unaffected by washing, dry cleaning, or aging. They are also wrinkle-resistant, machine-washable, quick-drying, and abrasion- and sunlight-resistant. They have dimensional stability and take dye easily. In interiors they are used mainly for curtains, and also for knit backings, and some rugs and carpets.

Saran

Saran fibers are noninflammable and resist weathering, rot, mildew, chemicals, staining, abrasion, and corrosion. Fabrics made of this yarn can be coated, laminated, shaped, or embossed. It can be washed with soap and water.

Fiberglass

Glass fibers are made by several companies and marketed under different names. Glass-fiber fabrics are noninflammable, will not shrink or stretch, and will not deteriorate in sunlight. They have low abrasion-resistance, no resilience, but can be made wrinkle-resistant and hang well. A superfine glass yarn is used in the making of curtains that may be either sheer or heavy and are of great serviceability (Fig. 9–5). Glass fabrics should never be dry-cleaned; they wash easily, and because they are non-absorbent, are dry when the water has run off.

FABRICS

WOVEN (TEXTILES)

Some fabrics are a combination of more than one weave. The Jacquard process, for example, combines weaves to produce fabrics with patterns that are generally in clear relief —that is, raised from the ground fabric.

The four basic weaves are plain, twill, satin, and gauze (or leno). In the plain weave, single threads pass alternately over and under each other. This weave is strong and, when made of tough fibers, can withstand rough use. Two variations of the plain weave are basket and rib weaves. In the former, more than one thread is used for warp and weft (the same number for both), and in rib weaves, either the warp or weft is a heavy thread and the other, light.

In twills each thread passes under one thread and over more than one (or vice versa), producing a texture of diagonal lines. Twills are usually more tightly woven than plain weaves; denim and serge are examples. In the satin weave much of the warp is left on the surface, making it smooth and lustrous. The gauze, or leno, weave is used for lightweight, open fabrics; in it the warp threads are twisted together around the filling (or weft) to prevent slipping.

There are several levels of weaves, but the final appearance or performance of a fabric is determined not only by the weave, but also by the construction, the balance between the number of warp yarns and filling yarns. An equal number of each makes a better-quality weave. Pile fabrics have two sets of warps: one forms a dense backing; the other is carried over a wire so that it forms a loop that stands away from the backing. The loops may be cut or left uncut. If cut, the result is velvet, plush, or similar, soft-surface material; if uncut, a frieze or terry cloth. Pile fabrics are very durable. The smoother ones spot easily, but can be processed for stain-resistance; the heavy ones are exceptionally sturdy and long wearing.

KNIT

Knitting produces fabrics that can be stretched in two directions. They are useful mainly for upholstery and slipcovers. Some curvilinear furniture uses such two-way-stretch fabrics to achieve a smooth fit. Some slipcovers (of knitted nylon) stretch to accommodate furniture dimensions (within certain limits) (Fig. 9–6). A type of heavy casement curtain material made from rayon in knit patterns is practical where an intermediate-weight material (neither sheer nor heavy) is wanted.

FELTED

All-wool felts made especially for upholstery are available in several colors and wear well. A felted material made of polyester and viscose rayon yarns hangs very well, comes in many colors, and is particularly suitable for curtains and table covers.

VINYLS

Vinyl "fabrics" are available in sheets (in plain colors, printed, tex-

9–6 Knit fabrics conform to the folded forms of a modern chair and ottoman.

tured, and/or embossed) and as "supported" vinyl (the vinyl sheet is laminated to a backing of true fabric). These vinyls are used for upholstery and wallcoverings (see Chapter 8), and although slightly stiffer than ordinary fabrics, are handled like any others. They are sturdy, flame-resistant, and can be wiped clean with a damp cloth.

GENERAL CONSIDERATIONS

In selecting fabrics for use in interiors, the designer must determine the answers to questions pertaining to durability, color stability, soil- and rot-resistance, ease of cleaning, flamma-

bility,[4] dimensional stability, and susceptibility to deterioration by sunlight.

Durability of a fabric is a function not only of fibers used (for both warp and filling), but also of the method of interlacing or joining these fibers: the tighter weaves are sturdier. Fading is brought about by exposure to sunlight and certain gases and by abrasion and cleaning.

Soil-resistant finishes are effective,

4. The recently amended Flammable Fabrics Act gives the Secretary of Commerce power to enforce flame-retardancy standards for fabrics. While standards are embodied in many state and local codes, entrance of the federal government into this area may signal further controls, with resultant changes in the manufacture of new fabrics

but limited, especially if a fabric is subjected to continuous hard use—in a commercial or institutional setting, for example. Professional-quality dry cleaning is essential in extending the life of a fabric.

Dimensional stability is vital where a fabric is subject to stress, as in a chair, where the weight of a seated person can strain upholstery or slip-cover seams and cause seam slippage. Wrinkling in upholstery may be caused by filling that does not have the proper backing. Dimensional stability is also important in hangings if sagging, shrinking, and shifting are to be avoided. A fabric will last longer and shift less if the warp and fill are of the same weight. Uneven absorption of moisture can produce wrinkling and sagging, so that where moisture is a significant factor, it is best to choose fibers—like glass, polyester, acrylic, linen, or modacrylic—that have little or no absorbability. Open-weave fabrics can be stabilized with leno construction (see above), which locks the filling yarns in place, thus minimizing shifting.

Fibers can be treated to retard flammability. Many such fibers will continue to burn only while flame is applied to them, a characteristic that meets the requirements of most building codes, which usually specify that a fabric must "not support combustion."

Wools can be mothproofed and some rayons can be made mildewproof. Some lining fabrics (such as Milium) used for curtains are coated with a resinated metal (usually aluminum) that gives them temperature-insulating properties. Scotchgard and Zepel, stain repellents, are effective against both water- and oil-borne stains, and withstand both laundering and dry cleaning. A wet stain can be blotted or rolled off fabrics so treated, and dried stains can be removed relatively easily; the accumulated grime of daily use, however, gradually wears into the fabric.

In selecting a fabric, the main basis is, of course, suitability, which includes esthetic aspects as well. Before selecting a fabric on the basis of appearance, however, it is vital to consider all other aspects, from durability to ease of maintenance. One must ask what function the fabric will perform; if curtains, for example, what kind? And to how much sun will they be exposed? If for upholstery, how is it to be used; to what degree and kind of wear will it be subjected? Upholstery fabrics cover cushions, padding, and webbing, and so must meet much more rigid standards of wear than slipcover fabrics. Upholstery fabrics are not removable, however, and so must have maintenance characteristics different from fabrics for slipcovers, which *can* be removed for cleaning.

BIBLIOGRAPHY

Encyclopedia of Textiles, by editors of *American Fabrics Magazine* (Prentice-Hall, 1960). Excellent reference book for every aspect of textiles. (New edition due 1972.)

HALLEN, NORMA, AND SADLER, JANE. *Textiles* (Macmillan, 1968). Well-organized, comprehensive information about fabrics.

POTTER, DAVID M., AND CORBMAN, BERNARD P. *Fiber to Fabric* (McGraw-Hill, 1967). Comprehensive, with good index. Includes fabric care information.

Threads of History—The American Federation of Arts: The Decorative Arts Program, 1965. The exhibition handbook; covers the history and use of fibers, including man-made fibers. Easy to read, informative.

10–1 Wood—in the wall paneling and furniture—is the dominant material in a modern conference room.

PRINCIPAL MATERIALS

The great variety of materials available today is a result not only of the development of synthetics, but of processes that have enhanced the quality and potentials of older materials. Most materials, including natural ones, are being changed constantly in an effort to improve them. Technologists have also discovered many ways to combine natural and synthetic materials, as well as devising unique ways of using them.

A designer must know and understand the basic nature, the potentialities, and the limitations of materials so that selection can be made on a basis of proven performance, as well as on appropriateness in terms of function and appearance. It is essential to check all known uses of a material in its actual application on specific jobs. Discussion with a manufacturer or his representative can often produce valuable information.

In the past, interior and exterior materials could be neatly separated; today, almost any exterior material may be found in some application in an interior.

NATURAL MATERIALS

WOOD

Probably the preferred and most commonly used material for interiors (and exteriors) is wood (Fig. 10–1).

Wood is readily available in many parts of the country, and is comparatively inexpensive, strong, durable, and easy to work. Almost all homes make some use of wood although other materials are replacing it to some extent in public and institutional buildings.

Woods are divided into two categories—hard and soft. Hardwoods come from broad-leaf, deciduous trees; softwoods from needle-bearing, coniferous trees, commonly known as evergreens.[1] Each wood has its own properties and appearance, the latter readily seen in the individual grain and color. Thus, wood combines warmth and individuality with flex-

1. *The Wood Handbook*, which provides complete data on the properties of wood, is available from the Forest Products Laboratory, Wisconsin State Department of Agriculture, Madison, Wis.

ibility in manufacture. While most untreated wood deteriorates on exposure to high humidity and water, this weakness is greatly minimized in plywood and other specially processed woods, and by various resistant finishes. Wood can be combined with plastic and metal for better wear, and processes have been developed that can make it virtually impervious to insects and decay.

Taken from the tree, wood is processed in a number of different ways, the simplest being to cut it into the various shapes and sizes needed for structural purposes—joists, beams, studs, and planks. Veneered wood (see Chapter 9), one of the special kinds of finished woods used in interiors, is composed of a thin layer of choice fine-grained wood (the veneer) bonded to a heavier piece, less choice and probably plywood. The veneer cuts used most are flat-slicing, quarter-slicing, and rotary. The use of veneer in an interior—whether in paneling or furniture—provides pattern that functions as a definite part of the overall design.

Plywood, which is stronger than solid wood, is made of an odd number of wood plies (layers) laminated with plastic resins under great heat and pressure. The grain of each ply is placed at right angles to that of the ply adjacent to it, so that the tendency of one layer to warp is counteracted by that of the other. Plywood—flat or curved is used for doors, walls, decorative paneling, and furniture. The top ply of plywood used for furniture or interiors is often given a special veneer finish.

The greatest weakness of natural wood used as a surface material in furniture is its susceptibility to abrasion, staining, and heat and moisture damage. Many processes exist that

produce surfaces resistant to such damage; woods so treated can have a finish anywhere from soft matte to high gloss. Finishes are graded according to resistance to staining (and to the effects of common household substances), to abrasion and impact resistance, to repairability, to fading, and to the effects of humidity and exposure. Some furniture will carry a certificate from a testing laboratory that rates the piece on the basis of these factors. Woods with special finishes are generally rated higher than plastics, and both are rated considerably higher than those with a conventional lacquer or varnish finish.

BRICK

Brick is used in a variety of ways, both in interiors (Fig. 10–2) and exteriors. It is the oldest man-made material—perhaps the earliest module —and is made of clay molded into blocks that are hardened by fire or sun. Unglazed brick may vary in color from deep red to light, or be many shades from tan to cream. Bricks can be glazed in any color. Face brick is made in special colors and shapes for a particular use.

Brick may be laid in different patterns, not only to strengthen the wall or bonding, but also to provide visual interest. The three most frequently used patterns are the *common bond,* in which every fifth or sixth row (course) consists of the ends (headers) of the bricks and the rest of the sides (stretchers); *English bond,* which is the same as common bond except that header and stretcher courses alternate regularly; and *Flemish bond,* in which headers and stretchers alternate within *each* course. Brick is used largely for walls and fireplaces in interiors.

10–2 Extensive use of brick in a home interior.

10–3   A rugged fieldstone wall
is a foil for the smooth surfaces
and textures of furnishings.

STONE

The use of stone for building and ornamentation probably began in pre-history. Most of the monumental buildings of the Western world were built of stone. Today, modern methods and mechanization have done much to keep the cost of stone reasonable. The life span of stone is longer than most competitive materials, and maintenance is minimal. It is a popular material for interiors as well as exteriors (Fig. 10–3).

Not all stones are suited to the same purpose. The designer must consider a stone from the standpoint of its appropriateness to the type of building and structural function, if any, desired appearance and surface texture, and the climatic and atmospheric conditions to which it will be subjected. Certain stones seem to suggest certain qualities. Granite, for example, suggests solidity, substance, and security, while marble suggests grace and style. Properly used, good stone is completely waterproof, wears better than most synthetic materials, is strong, and exhibits considerable individual character. The various kinds differ in their resistance to damage by heat, moisture, and abrasion. Most popular for interiors are granite, marble, slate, sandstone, and limestone.

Granite

Granite exists in more textures and varieties than any other stone, with a range of color that is almost equal to that of marble. It is strong and durable and is used in interiors where an imposing and stately effect is desired. Two of the finest modern buildings in New York are granite-clad—the Columbia Broadcasting System Building and the Whitney Museum of American Art. Because granite cannot be used in thin slabs, it is more expensive than marble.

Marble

Marble is limestone whose crystalline structure has been changed by pressure and great heat. It is considered an elegant stone, and is used extensively in interiors. It offers a wide range of colors, wears well, and is fairly easy to maintain, although it is susceptible to staining. It can be used in thin sheets as a veneer and can be processed to give finishes from high gloss to dull (Fig. 10–4).

Slate, Sandstone, and Limestone

Slate is used for floors and walls as well as for roofs. It is tough and brittle, with a very hard but easy to maintain surface. Sandstone is most commonly seen in the many brownstone houses built in the nineteenth century. It varies in color, from dull crimson through greenish brown to a bluish gray. The colors are particularly pleasant, the stone strong, though not as resistant as granite and marble to erosion by the elements. The many different kinds of lime-

10–4 Marble heightens the formal elegance of a symmetrical space.

stone, all of which weather well, require little maintenance. The best known kind in this country is Indiana limestone. Travertine, used for floors and on walls, is a limestone. Limestone is the most like marble of the other building stones.

CONCRETE

Concrete is a building material made by mixing cement, sand, gravel, and water to form a semifluid that becomes rock-hard when dry and "set." It can, therefore, be given innumerable shapes (according to the shape of the mold into which it is poured) and surfaces (by varying the mix). It is fireproof, exceptionally sturdy, and can withstand great pressure. For even greater strength, it can be reinforced with steel rods placed in the concrete before it has hardened. This reinforcing makes it possible to produce curved or cantilevered forms that are capable of supporting great weight. Forms may vary from a thin, 2- to 3-inch delicate shape to heavy, molded masses. Concrete can be covered with a veneer of brick, opaque glass, marble, metal, and some plastics. It is also cast into blocks, which are widely used for both interior and exterior walls, especially in inexpensive homes and many industrial and office buildings. Since the blocks, too, are formed in a mold, they can be varied in many ways.

A unique advantage of concrete is that it is usually designed for a specific structure and manufactured (poured into the wooden forms in which it hardens) on the site as part of the construction process.

GLASS

Glass as part of interior environment has increased rapidly in importance and variety of use since the end of the nineteenth century, when new structural methods made it unnecessary for walls to bear the weight of upper floors and roofs. Glass is basically the result of fusing silica sand, soda ash, limestone, salt cake, and certain incidental ingredients. The chief disadvantage of glass, of course, is that it is breakable in most forms, but there are some stronger varieties among the many new types of glass that have been developed and that have greatly increased its po-

tential for use in interiors (Fig. 10–5). Glass needs no upkeep except cleaning, and is impervious to water, grease, dirt, insects, and most acids.

The three most common types of glass are sheet (window), plate, and float. For window glass the manufacturing process is over when it has cooled; plate glass, much heavier, is made transparent by grinding and polishing. (Rough plate glass, often used for interior partitions, is unpolished, with a textured appearance, and is translucent.) Plate glass is available tinted to reduce sun heat, in a heat-absorbing form, and in a heavy-duty form made in 25-foot lengths. Float glass, a comparatively new development, is made by a process less costly than that of plate glass; their characteristics, however, are essentially the same.

Insulating glass consists of two or more pieces of glass separated by an air space, which acts as an insulator, limiting heat loss in winter and heat gain in summer. Spandrel glass, which is strong, opaque, and made in sunfast colors is used for walls. Patterned glass comes in a variety of colors and is used decoratively or to let in light while shutting off an unsightly view.

Safety glass is of three kinds. Laminated safety glass is two layers of glass with a sheet of plastic between. Early laminated safety glass was unsatisfactory, tending to discolor and weaken with age, but improved plastics now permit manufacture of a clear glass that will crack but not shatter, and will not discolor. The plastic layer can be treated so that it helps control glare and shuts out radiant heat. Heat-tempered plate glass is resistant to breakage and breaks into small grains that do not have sharp edges. It is used for sliding doors, in glass-wall entrances to many buildings, and in

store windows. Wired glass, which has a wire mesh embedded in a single layer of glass, is breakable but does not shatter.

Reflective glass is coated so that it has high heat reflectance and low light transmittance. With such glass, vision in daylight into an interior is limited, providing privacy, while one may see from the inside out with almost no hindrance. Insulating glass coated in this manner reduces solar heat again, important in air-conditioned spaces.

Quality mirrors are made of plate glass. Two-way mirrors, which act much like the reflective glass described above, can function as a mirror or a window depending on the intensity of the light on the viewer's side relative to the intensity on the other side. With the viewer looking through the glass into a relatively lighter room, it acts as a window; looking from the lighter side, the viewer sees a mirror. This two-way glass has many uses—in house and apartment doors that permit the occupant to see a caller, who cannot see in; in nurseries, where children can be observed without being disturbed; in viewing windows in clinics and hospitals; and in security windows in banks, police stations, department stores, and post offices.

Glass coated with a transparent metallic-oxide film will conduct electricity applied to the surface through wires that can be connected at the edge of the glass, out of sight in the frame of a window. The current can be used to create heat for defrosting or de-icing.

METALS

Ferrous (Iron-Containing)

Cast and wrought iron as well as steel and its alloys (with nickel for greater strength, or with chromium for hardness) are ferrous metals. Cast iron was the first substitute for wood or stone in building construction, and many of the early cast-iron products were made to look like wood or stone. In the second half of the nineteenth century, a number of magnificent buildings were erected in which pre-fabricated cast iron was used. Cast iron set the stage for steel skeleton construction with such buildings as the Crystal Palace, various railway stations in England, the Eiffel Tower, two large libraries in Paris, and some elegant industrial buildings in lower Manhattan, in New York City.

Steel made possible a strong but light form of contemporary building (see Chapter 2) that is exemplified in the designs of Mies van der Rohe. It can be cast or extruded (forced through a die) in many different sizes and shapes, solid or hollow. Today it is used not only for structural and functional purposes, but for decorative ones as well. It is also frequently used in combination with other materials in modern furniture.

Nonferrous

Aluminum, used in many interior areas as a window frame, is light-weight, watertight, corrosion- and fire-resistant, rust-, rot-, and termite-proof. It needs no paint to prevent oxidation and is not subject to swelling, splitting, or warping. It does not, however, provide the natural insulation of wood, and in colder climates, water may condense on it. Combined with other materials it is used for furniture and decorative objects (Fig. 10–6). Thresholds, stair treads, screening, windows, and doors of all kinds are made of aluminum. Moving parts in aluminum windows usually slide readily against each other. Sun-control devices, many kinds of blinds, and solar overhangs are practical in aluminum, as are movable interior partitions, with or without glass, which are available in a wide range of colors. Color can be imparted to aluminum by "anodizing," a process that produces a luminous, highly wear-resistant finish.

Although copper, zinc, tin, and lead are found less commonly in interiors, bronze, an alloy of tin and copper, has many uses. Brass, an alloy of copper and zinc, and not as strong as bronze, is often used for door-knobs, hardware, fireplace furniture, grills, and decorative objects.

PLASTICS

Plastics form a large and varied group of materials that, although solid in the finished state, at some stage in their manufacture can be made to flow (and thus be shaped) by the application of heat or pressure or both. Thus, all plastics are synthetic (produced by man by chemical synthesis), but not all synthetics are plastic.

There are two basic kinds of plastics: *thermoplastic*, which becomes soft when exposed to sufficient heat, then hardens when cooled, and *thermosetting*, which is given a permanent shape when heat or pressure is applied. The main thermoplastics used in interiors are: acrylic, used widely for rugs and textiles; nylon, also used for textiles and carpets; vinyl (which can be flexible or rigid),

10–6 Spare aluminum
furniture in an effective design
with upholstered pieces.

used for fabric, floor and wall coverings, and for coating materials. Thermosetting plastics used in interiors are: amino, made into dishes and laminates, the latter used with textiles and in table tops; polyester, used for textiles, rugs, carpets, interior partitions, and translucent panels for wall or ceiling; and polypropylene or olefin, which may be either thermoplastic *or* thermosetting and is produced as a fiber or a foam used for cushions, mattresses, rugs, carpets, and rug underlays.

Plastics are used widely for small functional objects, molded furniture, laminated table and counter tops, structural members in house frames, housings (as in electrical and mechanical apparatus), and even entire houses (Fig. 10–7). Good design requires that plastics look like plastics and not be an imitation of a natural material.

A peculiar advantage of plastics is that, being man-made, their characteristics can be tailored to their functions. Thus, because the particular properties of each plastic are known, it is feasible to make new combinations of plastics or of plastics with natural materials that will fulfill specific needs, and at the same time upgrade reliability, design, and performance while lowering costs. Plastics are also lightweight, do not deteriorate readily, can be made in a wide range of colors, and are adaptable to mass-production methods. Their use in furniture is now widespread. In some ways, plastics outperform wood. They can be tough, light, and waterproof, and generally will not split, warp, or swell. With plastics, once the mold has been made, it is easy and inexpensive to form complicated shapes. This has resulted in a flood of badly designed home furnishings.

10–7 Molded plastic furniture (*at left and opposite*) and structures of sprayed urethane foam (*below*).

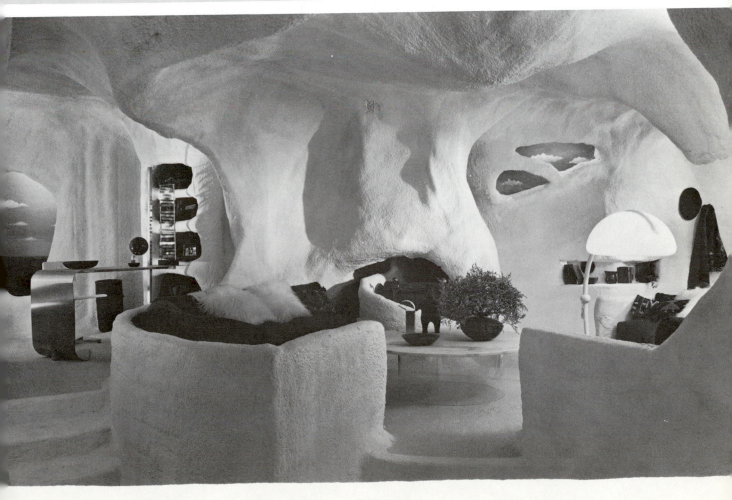

Irradiated plastic-impregnated wood is much harder than ordinary wood, more abrasion-resistant, and essentially splinter-proof, yet still absorbs moisture at much the same rate. It is also flame-resistant and mars can be sanded away because the tough plastic is not at the surface alone, but runs through the wood.

Plastic furniture may be of the molded or inflatable type. Chairs, sofas, and tables of both kinds are available. Molded pieces have been in use longer and have proven successful in some areas, particularly children's furniture. Some beautiful pieces have been made of acrylics. Clear plastic sheets (which sometimes scratch readily) are often used with wood or metal in tables and bookcases. The inflatable pieces can be sturdy and practical but can be punctured by sharp edges. Smaller pieces can be deflated for easy transportation and can be reinflated with a simple foot pump or a vacuum cleaner. Inflatable pieces have proven very satisfactory for use on boats.

Decorative plastic-laminated table and counter tops of many kinds and patterns are used commonly. Outdoor furniture that is weatherproof makes use of the advantages of plastics. Many such articles use vinyl-covered slats, tubes, or wood strips. Flexible urethane foam constitutes 60 percent of the stuffing material used in sofas and cushions. The manufacturer can tailor the characteristics of the foam to the degree of firmness, lightness, resiliency, and support needed.

ACOUSTICAL MATERIALS

Sound in an interior travels to the ear directly, or by reflection from room surfaces, or by both routes. Ordinary surfaces absorb little and reflect nearly all of the sound that strikes them. Acoustical materials must be selected on the basis of appearance, light-reflection, resistance to flame spread or penetration, durability, and ease of maintenance—as well as their sound-damping qualities.

The degree of acoustical control needed in an interior depends on the use of the space. The needs in an auditorium or lecture hall—audibility and minimal interfering sound—are not those of restaurants, offices, and factories, where control of undesirable noise, called sound conditioning, is the essential aim. In the first application the acoustical equipment is planned for the purpose of making speech and music readily heard and, in the case of music, with good fidelity. In the second application the essential function of acoustical treatment is to remove as much of the reflective noise as possible. Sound conditioning requires a greater amount of acoustical materials than simple acoustical control.

Since the largest surface in a room is usually the ceiling, it is generally covered entirely with acoustical material, which is often combined with a dropped ceiling of aluminum that incorporates lighting. Additional treatment may be applied to walls.

The basic physical property of acoustical materials that enables them to absorb sound is their porosity. When a sound wave enters a porous material, the air within the pores begins to vibrate; the resulting friction transforms part of the sound into heat. There are, however, several types of sound-absorptive materials. One has a hard, smooth surface that is perforated, and it is in the perforations that the sound is trapped. A second uses a thin membrane that is free to move on the surface, transforming the sound into mechanical energy. Another kind is continuously porous, with no smooth surface. Certain types of paint can be used on this last surface without affecting its function. A thin, foamed plastic is also available (in various colors and textures) that can be attached directly to a wall or ceiling.

BIBLIOGRAPHY

CALLENDER, JOHN HANCOCK. *Time-Saver Standards* (McGraw-Hill, 1967). Comprehensive handbook of architectural design information, including extensive coverage of materials.

GLOAG, JOHN, AND BRIDGEWATER, DEREK. A *History of Cast Iron in Architecture* (Allen and Unwin, 1948). Structural use of cast iron from its discovery, and a discussion of its potential. Well illustrated.

O'NEILL, HUGH. *Stone for Building* (Heinemann, 1965). Readable and authoritative.

PARKER, H. E., et al. *Materials and Methods of Architectural Construction* (Wiley, 1958). A general reference book on materials.

PETER, JOHN. *Aluminum in Modern Architecture* (Reynolds Metal Co., 1956). The many ways aluminum is used in modern architecture; includes some interiors.

SAYLON, HENRY H. *Dictionary of Architecture*, 6th ed. (Wiley, 1966). Handy, pocket-sized reference with clear explanation of materials and building terms.

WILSON, J. GILCHRIST. *Exposed Concrete Finishes* (Maclaren, 1962). The uses of concrete in interiors and exteriors.

11–1 Functional simplicity in the furniture of a Shaker office (*top*) and dining room (*below*).

11

Primitive furniture, as with the beginning forms of all functional objects, was largely a response to need, and had as its basis the observation of natural forms. The limitations imposed on the early designer by the characteristics of materials at hand—their strength, resistance to wear and weather, and the ease with which they could be worked—may to some extent still be reflected in the furniture forms of today.

The maker of early hand-crafted furniture usually interpreted the need, selected the material, and often constructed the piece himself. The Windsor chair, popular in England in the seventeenth century and adapted for use in this country in the eighteenth, is a product of such a system; it has a simple, fine design appropriate to its use and its material. The furniture made by the Shakers, a religious sect whose members came to this country from England in the late 1700's, provides another example of design in which simplicity of form and appropriateness to function and material are evident (Fig. 11–1). In

FURNITURE

spite of the Shaker belief that the sole purpose of every household object was utility, the suitability of their designs in terms of both function and material resulted in an austere perfection and beauty; esthetics need not be sacrificed to function.

Today handmade furniture is rare, with the exception of custom-designed pieces not made in quantity. But the work of the individual cabinetmaker is still very important in the creation of high-quality furniture where design and detail are concerned.

Contemporary homes tend less and less to be the once-in-a-lifetime investment that they were a few years ago, when furnishings were carefully selected to become heirlooms. In a time when a premium is put on mobility, there is less emphasis on permanence and durability. In the armed forces and in such organizations as the Peace Corps and Vista, and even in some modern business and educational establishments, furnishings are minimal and sometimes expendable since it may be more economical to throw away certain pieces of furniture or equipment than to ship them.

Inflatable furniture answers similar needs, and some is designed so that when deflated a piece fits into a specially designed case, which may itself double as a piece of furniture.

FURNITURE CATEGORIES

The classification "furniture" can be subdivided into those objects in or on which one rests, and those in or on which one puts things. In the first category, of course, are included "seating"—chairs, sofas, benches, and so on—and beds; in the second, known commercially as "tables and case goods," are tables, chests, cabinets, desks, and storage pieces.

SEATING

In comparatively recent years there have been many innovations in chair design. The great-grandparent of the comfortable, upholstered, loose-seat-

11–2 A bergère; the design
appeared during the reign of
Louis XV.

cushioned chair of today seems to have appeared in France in the eighteenth century, during the reign of Louis XV. Comfort in a chair is related to function: a chair that is comfortable for dining is not easy to relax in. Following the early Renaissance, chairs were designed increasingly for different functions and more comfort. The *bergère*, the first chair designed primarily for comfort, appeared while Louis XV was controlling court life in France (Fig. 11–2). It had closed sides, padded arms, and a loose seat cushion, usually made of down. The front was wide and the arms set back to accommodate ladies' paniered skirts. The chair legs and back were curved, the latter often in the shape of an inverted horseshoe.

A chair today may be, in effect, an abstract sculpture. The variety of types of design has increased immensely since the day when a chair had either an x base or four legs, with a seat, back, and perhaps arms. One of the first new concepts in chair design was that of Michael Thonet, a cabinetmaker in Germany in the early 1830's. He developed a revolutionary bending and laminating process for wood and, with it, created chair frames so attractive, light, and durable (Fig. 11–3) that they are still popular and being produced today in original and contemporary designs. One of the first industrial designers, as well as a cabinetmaker, Thonet foresaw the future need for mass production of furniture.

A chair designed by Mies van der Rohe in 1926 and influenced by Thonet's bentwood was made of polished metal tubing and based on a cantilever principle (Fig. 11–4). In a chair that Marcel Breuer designed in 1925, the frame is innovative, but there is a traditional separation of the

11–3 *Above,* a Thonet chair, an example of one of the earliest (nineteenth century) uses of bentwood in furniture; *at left,* as used today in a restaurant setting.

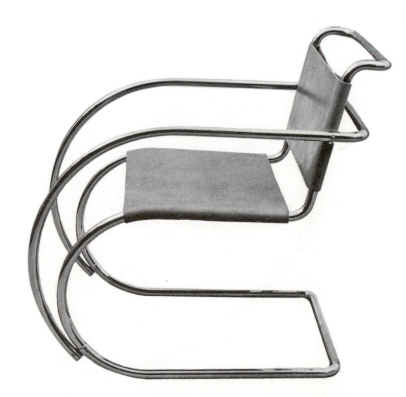

11–4 A Mies van der Rohe chair of metal tubing, designed in 1926.

supporting frame from the seat and back, both of which are made of stretched canvas. These solutions make optimal use of their materials.

The "Barcelona chair," designed by Mies for the International Exhibition in Barcelona in 1929, simple as it is, is technologically a masterpiece, using, as it does, the cantilever principle and taking advantage of the elasticity of the metal of the curved legs and back (Fig. 11–5). The chaise longue designed by Le Corbusier in 1927 (Fig. 11–6) was another innovation and is certainly the ancestor of a wide range of similar designs today, many of them made for use in the sun. In 1934 laminated plywood was used for frame, seat, and back in a chair designed by Alvar Aalto. The

Hardoy chair, with unique metal frame, which supports a seat and back of a heavy material, usually canvas or leather, was introduced in 1938 (Fig. 11–7).

Charles Eames' first molded laminated-plywood chair was made in 1946. This chair grew out of one Eames designed with Eero Saarinen that won a competition organized by the Museum of Modern Art in 1940–41. Facilities for manufacturing such a chair were not then available and, following the Second World War, after considerable experiment in designing furniture and in the technique of molding wood, Eames succeeded in completing this chair. With its molded plywood and metal rod frame, it represented another case

11–5   The cantilever principle used in Mies van der Rohe's "Barcelona chair" (1929).

11–6   A chaise longue designed by Le Corbusier in 1927.

11–7   The Hardoy chair, introduced in 1938; leather on a metal frame.

11–8 Metal rod and molded plywood in Eames' 1956 design (*above*) was later elaborated and fitted with cushions (*below*).

where a new form resulted from a new process. The process made it possible to mass-produce a chair that was inexpensive, light, comfortable, and sturdy; the principles involved in its construction have had a strong influence on chair design of the last twenty-five years.

In 1956 Eames applied molded-plywood techniques to a lounge chair and ottoman, and later used them in an armchair (fitted with downfilled leather cushions) that has become a modern classic (Fig. 11–8) in luxury seating and continues to be popular for home or office use.

Harry Bertoia, well-known sculptor, is the designer of a chair that resembles sculpture (Fig. 11–9). Made

of wire welded and shaped into an open mesh and lined with covered foam rubber, the whole is supported on a framework of metal rod. Another chair having considerable influence on modern chair design (Fig. 11–10) is that by Eero Saarinen (1957). It has a cast-aluminum pedestal base and fiberglass-reinforced, molded-plastic seat.

The simple Danish chairs made in the 1940's were less innovative but had strong influence in this country. Finn Juhl and Hans Wegner made some of the earliest designs; Jens Risom continues to produce furniture based on the Danish concept that is widely used today (Fig. 11–11). His chairs are simple, with wood used in a

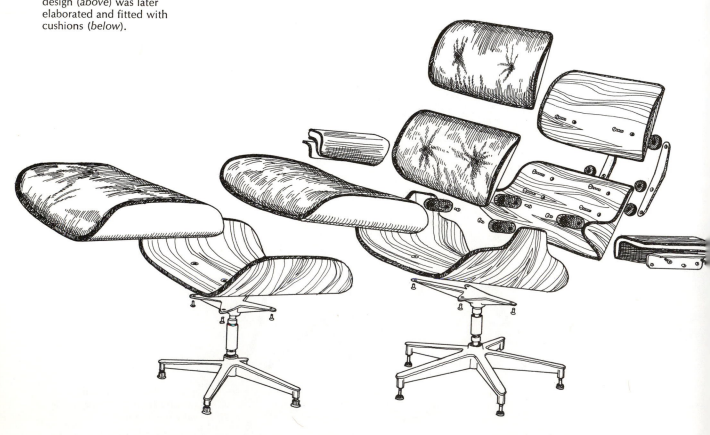

11–9 Bertoia's welded wire and rod chair, which used a foam rubber cushion.

11–10 Saarinen's fiberglass and molded plastic chair, designed in 1957.

11–11 Subtly sculptured wood in a Jens Risom chair.

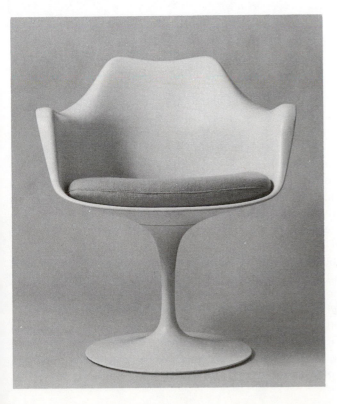

11–12 A chair utilizing some
of the new, simplified
techniques of upholstery.

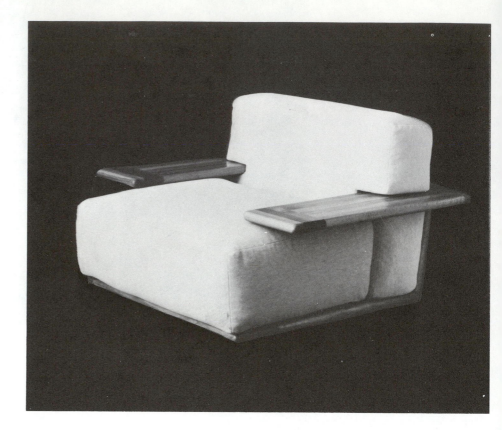

natural state, the surfaces sculptured and with a soft, low-gloss finish that is as lasting as harder kinds. Risom's view is that chairs should be suitable in function and appearance but not demand a great deal of attention in the general scheme.

The familiar upholstered chair has a frame, webbing, cushioning or filling, and covering and may also have coil or flat springs. Where wood is the material, mortised, tongue-and-groove, or doweled joints (used with corner blocks and modern bonding materials) will yield a sturdy frame. A traditional way of supporting a seat is with webbing. Filling will usually be of feathers or feathers-down combinations covered with ticking or plastic or rubber foam. The finest filling is a mixture of 80 percent goose

down plus feathers. Good cushions can be made of down and feathers in equal parts. Feathers may also be combined with foam rubber, latex, polyurethane, dacron fiber fill, or other synthetics, without springs. For chairs having a tight (attached) seat and back, filling is used to upholster the entire chair; with a loose seat or a loose back cushion, the chair proper requires less filling since the cushions provide adequate padding. Seams in the chair covering may be welted. Often a chair is covered with muslin and fitted with a slipcover that can be taken off for easy cleaning.

The traditional method of upholstering around a rigid frame has been enormously simplified in the past decades and is still undergoing improvement and simplification (Fig.

11–12). In some contemporary chairs a foam material with a finishing fabric laminated to it is bonded to a molded seat or back, or both. Molded-plywood and plastic chairs often have loose seat cushions usually of fabric-covered foam. Chairs, sofas, and day-beds may consist simply of a frame with legs (some also have a frame for seat back), with a wood or spring plat-form for seat cushions; these and the back cushions are usually made of foam cut to fit and covered with fabric. New elastic and springy materials are coming into use, such as a neoprene sheeting that can be stretched between two supports and, with the addition of a foam cushion, affords all of the softness of the earlier, thicker, more complicated seats.

In contemporary open-plan interiors, chairs are less frequently placed against a wall, and so most must now look attractive from every angle. With respect to how a chair will be seen in an interior, one must consider what its appearance will be both occupied and unoccupied, and how it will be affected by its background. In testing a chair for comfort, it is important not only to sit in it but to change position while sitting. Chairs with rigid seats, of course, do not adjust to the body as easily as those with some resilience.

TABLES AND CASE GOODS

In view of the diversity of tables available (Fig. 11–13), from antique step tables to modern plastic cubes, there can be little reason for selecting the wrong kind.

Heights of tables vary from about 15 inches, a convenient height for a coffee table, to 28 or 30 inches, com-fortable for dining. Card tables and desks are usually 28 or 29 inches high. When a table of any kind is to be used with chairs, the heights of the two should be coordinated; at least five inches should be allowed between the chair seat and the underside of tables. Where a multipurpose table is needed, drop-leaf tables are practical, as are console tables with leaves. (With this type of console, space for the storage of extra leaves must be planned.) A coffee table with sharp corners is not practical where space is limited; round tables are less likely to inflict bruises. Tables that hold lamps should have good stability, and their height, together with that of the light, should be related to that of nearby chair or sofa arms. Game tables that are to be used frequently should be planned as a permanent part of the furniture scheme.

A desk may be simply a table, or it may have storage space. It should have all the features of a good table as described above. Space for writing and for books or papers should be ample. Chests and cabinets may be low or fairly high, with two or more drawers. A cabinet is a storage piece with doors, usually with shelves inside. Bookcases and bookshelves—unless special-purpose—should have dimensions adequate for the majority of books, which range in size from about 4 x 7 to 8 x 11 inches.

Today's mass market has encouraged design of a versatile range of storage units (Fig. 11–14)—particularly, interchangeable units that allow for great flexibility in arrangement. Among the early designs of such *modular* furniture were those by George Nelson, whose "storage wall" (with some additions and modifications) is still in use. Cases such as

11–13 Tables—from the eighteenth to the twentieth centuries.

11–14 An arrangement of modular, interchangeable storage and desk units.

these included shelves, cabinets, chests of drawers, and work units, including desks. Such components, made today by many companies, can be combined in a variety of ways: some are hung on wall rails, others against a free-standing framework or on poles. There are styles and modular sizes for every kind of interior—residential, commercial, or institutional.

MATERIALS

Changes in design concepts and the many new kinds of furniture have brought about a great variety of new manufacturing techniques. In general, these techniques are associated specifically with the materials used: wood, rattan, metal, plastic, and the various cushioning materials or coverings—fabric, leather, or plastic. Although no one material is best for all furniture, the material most commonly used is wood.

Mahogany and walnut are two of the finer furniture woods. Maple, ash, and the harder varieties of birch wear well and resist denting. Gumwood and softer birch are strong but have less distinctive grains and are often used in combination with a veneer (a thin outer layer) of handsomer woods. Each kind of furniture wood —solid, plywood, and veneered—has its own suitability: solid wood for structural parts and areas that are to be carved, plywood for its great strength relative to weight, and veneers where matching of grains is desired. Veneer panels (made by gluing thin sheets of choice wood onto plywood) can be costly or inexpensive depending on the techniques used. There are certain disadvantages to wood as a furniture material. Solid wood is inclined to warp and may swell or crack. The supply of fine hardwoods is gradually being depleted and so its cost continues to rise. Mass-production techniques require highly standardized, uniform materials, and the composition of natural materials, like wood, tends to be variable.

Plastics have been in use for some time for upholstery coverings, in table tops, and as cushioning material. They are also combined with wood for

11–15   Rattan furniture in a design with upholstered pieces.

greater strength and wearability. Furniture made partially or entirely of plastic is accounting for a growing share of the furniture industry's sales volume. Distinctive furniture is being made from colorless or colored transparent and opaque plastic, such as acrylic, and printed and textured vinyl and polyester films can be laminated to molded plastic or inexpensive wood panels to produce finished surfaces.

Rattan, traditionally used for summer and porch furniture, is now being used in sturdier, more sophisticated pieces that have a variety of finishes and that employ varied seating materials and fine fabrics (Fig. 11–15). The finishes and fabrics are particularly suitable for simple, modern forms and are also being used in

11–16 Polished chrome and brass give a modern table and chairs a reflective dimension.

styles reminiscent of some traditional periods. Rattan furniture is suitable for almost any room in a home, as well as for offices, schools, and institutional buildings.

Metal is used in furniture of all kinds. Techniques for shaping tubing, metal rods, and wire, and agents for bonding metal to wood, glass, and plastics have made possible new and exciting pieces of furniture (Fig. 11–16). A table, for example, with a leather-covered top, may have stainless-steel legs, a bronze apron, and square bronze legs. Aluminum is also being used in tables, chairs, and case goods. While steel and aluminum in their natural state can enhance a design, they can also be permanently finished in many colors.

Although paper furniture must still be considered disposable and is not for permanent, quality construction, it seems promising and appears to be a much more versatile material than had been realized. Besides the advantage of its easy workability, it can be made waterproof, fireproof, and quite rigid.

Although the Federal Trade Commission and other government agencies exercise some control over the materials and processes of furniture manufacture, and materials used usually must be listed on each piece, it remains necessary for the designer to be alert and informed. Manufacturers' representatives can be helpful in determining the caliber of design and the quality of furniture.

BIBLIOGRAPHY

ASH, DAVID. *Dictionary of English Antique Furniture* (Miller, 1970). Easy to use and well illustrated.

ARONSON, JOSEPH. *The Encyclopedia of Furniture*, 3rd rev. ed. (Crown, 1965). Comprehensive, but organization has shortcomings, and drawing quality is inconsistent.

BOGER, LOUISE ADE. *The Complete Guide to Furniture Styles* (Scribner's, 1959). Easy-to-use, authoritative reference for furniture and decorative objects, starting with ancient Egypt. Excellent line drawings.

BRACKET, OLIVER. *English Furniture Illustrated*, rev. and ed. by H. Clifford Smith (Macmillan, 1950). Brief text. Fine photographs of English furniture from Gothic times to mid-nineteenth century.

CHIPPENDALE, THOMAS. *The Gentleman and Cabinet Maker's Director* (Dover, 1966). Edition as published in London in 1762 is filled with design ideas. Many illustrations.

DAVIDSON, MARSHALL B., ed. *The American Heritage History of Antiques from the Civil War to World War I* (American Heritage, 1969). Comprehensive coverage of a bewildering collection of styles from a rarely covered period. Excellent illustrations.

GLOAG, JOHN. *A Social History of Furniture Design from 1300 B.C. to 1960 A.D.* (Crown, 1966). Social developments in relation to furnishings. Fine illustrations from rarely seen private collections.

———. *The Chair: Its Origins, Design and Social History* (Barnes, 1967). Design and use of chairs since 1400 B.C.

HARRIS, EILEEN. *The Furniture of Robert Adam* (Tiranti, 1963). Short but well organized, and unique in its concentration on the furniture rather than the architecture of Robert Adam. One hundred and fifty-six illustrations.

HARRIS, JOHN. *Regency Furniture Designs* (Quadrangle Books, 1961). Brief text, many illustrations, all from contemporary Regency sources.

HINCKLEY, F. LEWIS. *A Directory of Antique Furniture* (Bonanza, 1953). Easy-to-use reference covering European and American furniture. Brief text discusses the spread of English and French design influences to other countries. More than 1000 photographs.

MARGON, LESTER. *Masterpieces of European Furniture* (Architectural Book Publishing, 1968). Beautiful photographs (with descriptive commentary) and more than four dozen measured drawings of European furniture from twenty-one European and two United States museums. Antipathy to modern styles does not detract from usefulness.

Modern Chairs, 1918–1970 (The Whitechapel Art Gallery, 1970). Arranged by the Circulation Department, Victoria and Albert Museum. Comprehensive and informative account of the evolution of modern chair design since 1918. Pictures of chairs by ninety designers.

NELSON, GEORGE. *Chairs* (Whitney, 1953). Brief account of the evolution of the chair; examines most of the innovative designs. Recommended for reference; good illustrations.

———. *Storage* (Whitney, 1954). Photographs of a wide variety of shelving, unit cases, and special-purpose and architecturally designed storage units. Captions identify room designer of storage pieces.

NOYES, ELIOT F. *Organic Design in Home Furniture* (Museum of Modern Art, 1969). Furniture design in the thirties and early forties. Many photographs and drawings (including those of details of construction).

WAYWARD, HELENA, ed. *World Furniture* (McGraw-Hill, 1965). Comprehensive, fully illustrated history of furniture (with interiors) from Egypt to the present. Includes material by twenty-five experts.

12

In an interior design, the term *accessory* refers to an object that enhances the design. Each such piece should add to the functional and/or esthetic effectiveness of another element—a wall, a piece of furniture, a fireplace—and, thus, will be important to the design, helping to give it character. Where the design can have a personal character, as in a home or private office, the accessories may express the personality of the person or persons who are to use the space. Accessories can also be utilized to complete or highlight an aspect of a design (Fig. 12–1a), emphasize a color (Fig. 5–4), add interest (Fig. 12–1b), or simply to invite attention to a certain area (Fig. 12–1c).

Accessories may be major or minor factors, according to their prominence and meaning to the client. There are few valid rules for selecting them. They should have quality and appropriateness, and should never compete with other parts of a design.

The proper placing of accessories is at least as important as their selection. Too many isolated objects are likely to become clutter. When several objects are used together, proper emphasis is important. The eye should go instinctively to whatever is featured, and the rest should be subordinate. Space between objects is a part of the design. Emphasis, contrast, variety, rhythm, and balance are as important in the use of accessories as they are in a whole design.

Although there is some overlapping of categories, accessories can be divided into: (1) those used for purely esthetic reasons, and which qualify as works of art, such as sculpture, paintings or drawings (in any medium), a hanging, or a choice antique; (2) functional objects that may also be beautiful, such as clocks, fireplace and desk equipment, mirrors, ashtrays, and containers of various kinds—for flowers or candy, for example (Fig. 12–2); (3) simple decorative objects, such as a piece of driftwood or rock crystal, or a seashell; (4) plants, indoor trees, and flowers.

In the case of the first category, the diversity of subject, color, medium, and technique make it particularly easy to find objects suitable to the total design. As with any element

ACCESSORIES

of a design, frames should be selected with respect to scale, proportion, color, and perhaps decoration on the frame. Good proportion is also important in the dimensions of a mat and in the relationship of the mat, picture, and frame. Whatever is hung on the wall should be harmonious with the space where it is hung. Proper lighting adds much to the effectiveness of art objects and should be designed to enhance them.

Sculpture accessories may include many varied objects—a small marble figure, a huge metal mobile, a wood carving, a ceramic or stone piece. The dimensionality of wall reliefs is more effective than pictures in those spaces where a strong play of light and shadow is desirable. Background and lighting are important to the satisfactory viewing of any sculpture. Again, each piece should be visually integrated into the overall scheme.

The diversity of objects in the second and third categories is reflected in the materials of which they are made. Ceramic, however, is one of the materials more commonly used. Ceramics include all ware made

of clay shaped and hardened by heat. Pottery and earthenware are made from coarse clays fired at a lower temperature than other ceramics, and are heavy, soft, porous, and opaque. Usually thinly glazed, they are easily broken and rarely waterproof. Stoneware is somewhat finer and is fired at a higher temperature than pottery and earthenware. It holds its shape during firing, is nonporous, waterproof, and hard. It is made in white or colors, and some early pieces, still in use, have a distinctive, lustrous brown glaze. Porcelain is the finest ceramic. Made of a special clay fired at a high temperature, it is nonporous and has a hard, high-gloss glaze. It can be translucent and is more resistant to chipping than the other ceramics. What is commonly called china today is sometimes porcelain and sometimes a glazed ceramic that has some, but not all of the qualities of porcelain.

The different kinds of stone, from highly polished marble to rough-cut fieldstone, used in a wide variety of forms—containers, sculpture, wall surfacing, among others—provide an-

12–1   Accessories used to highlight a design (*opposite*), add interest (*left*), and focus attention (*right*).

12–2   An interior in which some accessories are functional.

12–3 Lighted niches display
a collection to advantage
in a living room.

other means of adding variety and interest by the use of accessories. Colors of marble range from pure white to a black that is virtually solid, and there are many different kinds of veining and clouding patterns. Granite, sandstone, slate, limestone, and some rarer stones contribute their distinctive textures and colors.

Silver, pewter, gold, bronze, brass, copper, steel, aluminum, and iron are used alone and in combination with each other or with materials such as wood, glass, leather, or plastic. Accessories of metals such as copper and brass give an impression of warmth. Both brass and copper have definite

colors, which should be considered with the other colors in the design. Silver is cooler, while pewter's gray tone is relatively warm. Aluminum accessories in their natural color are quite cool in effect; the metal, however, is also available in various anodized colors (Chapter 10). Fireplace furnishings, usually of metal, are particularly important as accessories since most fireplaces are the visual focal point of a room.

Wood and leather accessories have their own special qualities: they are familiar, pleasant to the touch, warm in winter, and cool in summer. Leather—warm, soft, and rich—is used

mainly in desk accessories, waste-
baskets, various containers, and small
art objects.

Glass and some plastic accessories
have certain qualities in common:
both can be transparent or translucent, plain or colored, and shiny or
matte finished. In general, well-designed plastics are more expensive
than glass, but are less fragile.

Also in the category of decorative
objects are collections of a kind that
can be exhibited in a visually attractive way, and include such things as
travel mementos and sentimental
treasures. Interesting and well arranged, they can add character to a
room. Small collections can be displayed in bookcases or hanging
shelves, or framed. For larger collections, cabinets, cupboards, or special
brackets are practical. A collection
should be well lighted and harmonize
with its background (Fig. 12–3).

Potted plants (including small
trees), flowers, arrangements of leaves
(fresh or dried) and branches or dried
natural forms are also used in accessory roles. Flower and leaf arrangements are of many kinds, from the
highly stylized and painstaking Japanese method to the most casual of
groupings. Living plants, of course,
require maintenance, the cost of
which should be considered in operations budgets. Planters are available
in many styles including well-designed
architectural pottery containers. Used
singly or in groups, plants should be
arranged so that the line of their top
edge relates well to the area or background and to the line of parts of
plants that hang over the edge. The
texture of the foliage, the shape of the
leaves, and the way they grow from
the stem should be considered in the
design.

BIBLIOGRAPHY

BERNIER, G., AND R., eds. *Aspects of Modern Art; The Selective Eye: An Anthology of Writings on Modern Art* (Reynal). Modern art through the School of Paris. A genuine aid to understanding it.

BOGER, L. A., AND H. B. *The Dictionary of Antiques and the Decorative Arts* (Scribner's, 1957). Excellent refer-ence, with authentic and handsome drawings.

California Design of Nine (Cunning-ham Press, 1965). Objects used in interiors, from the purely decorative to furniture and products of indus-trial design. Excellent photographs in color and black and white.

CLARK, KENNETH M. *Looking at Pictures* (Holt, Rinehart and Winston, 1960). Analysis of sixteen great paintings. The introduction may be helpful to a client making his own selection.

COX, WARREN E. *The Book of Pottery and Porcelain*, Vols. I and II (Crown, 1970). Comprehensive, covering both materials and history.

GOMBRICH, E. H. *The Story of Art* (Phaidon, distributed by New York Graphics Society; paperback: Oxford University Press, 1966). A discrim-inating narrative account of people and events from art history. Useful to clients selecting works of art for an interior.

HAEDEKE, HANNS-ULRICH. *Metalwork* (Universe, 1970). The development of metalwork within changing social settings.

LOWRY, BATES. *The Visual Approach Experience* (Abrams, 1960). A fas-cinating guide to observing, under-standing, and appreciating a work of art.

MCILHANY, STERLING. *Art as Design, Design as Art* (Reinhold, 1970). A unique collection that poses a chal-lenge to the overcritical or undis-criminating.

13

Experiments have proved that a person in a congenial environment functions more constructively than one living in a disagreeable or frustrating setting. A home should be a haven that provides satisfaction for each person living in it. Practical esthetics can achieve this.

In planning shelter for living—whether a large house or a tiny apartment, whether in city, farm area, or small town—the first and most important step is to determine very specifically the kind of home wanted by the user. Thus, a home should be planned to meet the needs and tastes of the occupants, while conforming to high standards of design. The project may cover the improvement of an existing home or the planning of a new one. Whichever it is, it should be considered—as described in Chapter 4, *The Planning Process*—from all angles, first as a whole, then each room individually.

The variety of techniques in home construction today is enormous. The house as a separate and private structure is still considered by many to be the ideal living space. Size may range from spacious rooms in an expensive home to a relatively few square feet in a tiny prefabricated house. Real-estate development houses and federal, state, and municipal housing projects offer in vast numbers another kind of home. Huge complexes composed of residential buildings that incorporate their own shopping, utility, and recreational centers are being erected, and according to a federal housing survey, the mobile home constituted about half of all single dwellings purchased in a recent twelve-month period.

Many new concepts for housing are being developed. In the next few decades, some of these, now in the experimental stage, will become commercially feasible. Structures made by spraying inflatable forms with concrete, fiberglass, or plastic are appearing. New techniques of construction are suitable for single dwellings or apartment towers: concrete boxes stacked by helicopter, used to make townhouses; fold-out boxes stacked on poles; spun-glass cocoons; insulated boxes of fiberglass, usable as small dwellings or single rooms;

THE DWELLING

"supercubes," now in production, which contain separate areas for conversation, dining, dressing, and an office, include all necessary furniture as part of the unit, and with modifications can be made into a play area, a space for guests, or a minimum kit for living. In France a "total homestead" is being tried out that is 19 x 19 feet and contains living space, toilet, shower, washbasin, air conditioning, and its own lighting source.

In the United States in 1970, a government-sponsored program ("Breakthrough") was begun, the aim of which was to develop attractive, functional housing that could be mass-produced. Twenty-two companies have built or are building pilot projects of their proposals.

Since the Second World War, building in the United States has accounted for about 10 percent of the gross national product. The spectrum is vast, with a greatly expanded sense of the use of space and the materials and techniques available. The familiar materials—wood, stone, steel, concrete, glass, and aluminum—are serving their old uses, plus many new

ones. Reinforced and prestressed concrete, structural steel, and laminated wood can span great distances. The use of plastics, alone or combined with other materials, is growing at a phenomenal rate. Fiberglass is being used in new ways, alone and in combination with other materials. New materials pioneered in aerospace technology are rot-proof, fire-retardant, waterproof, and immune to termite damage, and have a potential in construction. Polyurethane foam is being tried for house shells and walls.

Industrialized housing, which includes systems using factory-fabricated components that are completely or partially assembled and finished at the factory, is coming to provide a wider variety of design within a specified price range than is possible with on-site building methods. These industrialized techniques can mean pre-assembled sections—walls and roofs, for example—or even complete rooms. Such items as packaged kitchens, baths, and utility cores (containing plumbing, heating, and wiring) are being used.

Although all of the systems are

13–1   Exterior space used functionally at Safdie's "Habitat."

package shipped to the site, consists of three-dimensional, wood-frame, sectionalized modules. The modules provide structural frames, which are arbitrary as far as floor plan is concerned. Flexibility is provided by three kinds of diverse components that can be used interchangeably in certain specified areas: slide-out elements such as projecting windows, balconies, closets, skylights, and foyers; fold-out elements such as pitched roofs, balconies, and porches; and add-on elements such as entrances, porches, decks, screen walls, balconies, parapets, and awnings.

In theory, everyone is free to choose the kind of home he wants; actually, standardization limits the choice in all except the most expensive homes. For economic reasons the trend to standardization is likely to increase. In addition, the growing use of mass-production methods often stresses function at the expense of appearance. To most people, however, home is a particular place, created for oneself, or oneself and family, and architects and interior designers are searching for better ways that will permit investment of every new dwelling with this personal spirit of living. It is in low-cost housing that it is most difficult to realize these ideals.

Public housing programs, in particular, are limited by cost factors, so that spaces in them tend to be too small and improperly scaled. To alleviate such aspects, designers are learning to expand space visually by making functional use of exterior space (Fig. 13–1), for example, without loss of privacy or function and without added cost.

When a dwelling and its surroundings are in harmonious relationship, each is enhanced by the other. Old New Orleans, one example from the

termed industrialized housing, there are two basic kinds—open and closed. In the open system, reinforced-concrete wall and floor panels, precast in a factory near a building site, are erected on that site by power crane. Windows, doors, plumbing, electrical conduit, and any special features are incorporated at the plant. However, the floor plan can be determined at the site and all subsystems designed and subcontracted separately, thus allowing for flexibility in planning. In the closed system, a totally designed

13–2 Interior of an old
New Orleans home.

past of fine coordination of interior and exterior environment (Fig. 13–2), created a living area that came close to fulfilling the ideal total residential environment that designers are striving for today. James Marston Fitch considers that the features of this New Orleans architecture show an understanding of the "local relationship between climate and comfort, and an intelligent use of a limited range of simple materials and techniques to manipulate the relationship."[1] Some of the features of this coordination: living areas elevated so as to avoid flooding and insects and to take advantage of prevailing breezes; huge parasol-type roofs and continuous porches and balconies to protect against subtropical rain and sun; and large doors and windows, high ceilings, ventilated attics, central halls, and the louvered jalousie— all to maximize coolness in the warm climate (the last, while maintaining privacy).

Twentieth-century designers of environment have emphasized the importance of the person, and particularly of the human body, with its characteristic needs and dimensions, as the first consideration in planning any kind of dwelling. Laszlo Moholy-Nagy constantly reminded his Bauhaus students that man, not the product, is the end to be kept in view. Frank Lloyd Wright planned his houses to fit an average-size man, believing in no other scale. Le Corbusier's modular system (see Chapter 2) of dimensioning was based on the figure of his "ideal" man. The relationship of the human body to the dwelling must underlie all planning.

1. James Marston Fitch, *Architecture and the Esthetics of Plenty* (New York: Columbia University Press, 1961), p. 244.

PLANNING THE DWELLING [2]

Many homes are planned with separate zones for different activities— playroom, work or sewing room, and so on. More often, multipurpose rooms, tailored to fit family needs are economical and practical (Fig. 13–3). A kitchen may double as a family room, although surveys show that the separate family room is most popular. Differences in waking hours increase the use of some areas, the young, for example, using a space at earlier hours, and older persons, later. If space permits, a room can be used for quiet work, and another, at a proper distance, for noisier activities. It is sometimes possible to locate convenient storage areas so that they also work as sound buffers. When possible, zones should be carefully worked out with a family before the floor plan is started.

In planning zones in interior space, whether house, apartment, or trailer, it is important to know if existing furnishings are to be used and what these will be. The activity needs for each room, as they reflect the interests and tastes of those who will use the rooms, must be considered. Do they prefer formality or informality; bright, clear colors or soft, subtle ones; simplicity or elaboration; delicate or sturdy furniture?

A brief analysis of the specific needs and functions of the home, room by room is necessary. General living and leisure activities must, of course, be given first consideration. Good spatial arrangement of functional areas—entrance, kitchen, bath,

2. The application (in the planning process) of the background material on the dwelling, presented here and on subsequent pages, is described in Chapter 4, *The Planning Process*.

13-3 *Above*, conventional family living room. *Below*, example of multipurpose room in which a book corner and writing desk become a dining area.

13–4 *At left,* dining and cooking areas combined; *at right,* dining in a separate, more formal setting.

utilities and storage—can contribute a great deal to smooth functioning in a home. Although the time spent in dining and sleeping areas is not as great as that spent in others, their special purpose must also be recognized in the planning.

Whether or not the entrance is a separate room, it should have an atmosphere of welcome with a convenient place for outer clothing. Guests like to check their appearance on arrival, hence a mirror is desirable in that area.

The living room, usually the area most used in a home, should be a center for conversation, where several people can be comfortably seated. If the room is large enough, there may be a secondary grouping; if not, additional seating pieces should be provided that are light enough so they can be moved into the circle of conversation, should there be additional

guests. Space is needed for relaxing and reading, music (performing and/ or listening), television viewing, games, and so on. Some living rooms may include facilities for dining—for example, an expandable console or a drop-leaf table. In small homes or apartments, a portion of the living room may also be needed for play space for a small child or for a baby's playpen.

The function of a dining room (Fig. 13–4) is simple: to permit its occupants to eat in comfort. This may require storage or serving space. A table is commonly centered in a dining room, but rectangular tables may be placed with either a side or end against a wall.

Bedrooms usually have as a function dressing as well as sleeping. They are the most personal rooms in a dwelling, and it is there that an individual can indulge his preferences in furniture, arrangement, and decoration. Since comparatively little time is spent in most bedrooms outside of sleeping hours, space allotted to them may be comparatively small; they should be located in a quiet part of the house or apartment.

Food is prepared and stored in one of five kinds of kitchens: (1) the small efficiency unit, which is not a separate room, with all utilities occupying minimal space and usually more or less concealed by a screen or partition of some kind; (2) a complete but small room, with all utilities, but little other space; (3) a larger room with utilities, storage, and counter space (Fig. 13–5); (4) a room large enough to contain facilities for eating meals, as well as cooking and storage; (5) an area like that described in (4) but in the open-plan style (Fig. 13–6), open to and partaking of other living space. The kitchen needs standard equipment and appliances, adequate counter space, and an exhaust fan, which contributes to both comfort and cleanliness. Stove, sink, and refrigerator should be placed to minimize walking and maximize convenience; this usually requires that the sink be placed between the other two. Counters beside the sink are useful in both preparing food and cleaning up. When open, the refrigerator door should not interfere with other doors. Electrical outlets should be placed for convenience in operation of appliances.

Storage cabinets and shelves are available in a great variety of designs. Drawers should have stops to prevent them from being pulled all the way out, and shelves should be adjustable.

A bathroom can be minimal—totally functional—or luxurious (Fig. 13–7). It may be largely prefabricated, containing the simplest fixtures, or

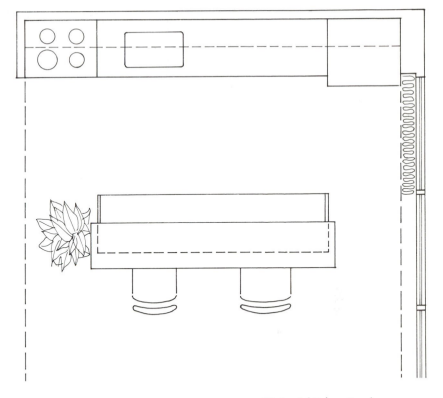

13–5 A kitchen (in plan, *above*) with utility and storage space and a cafeteria-type counter for dining.

13–6 Full kitchen (in plan, *above*) whose open-plan spaces merge with those of dining area (foreground). Note food-preparation "island."

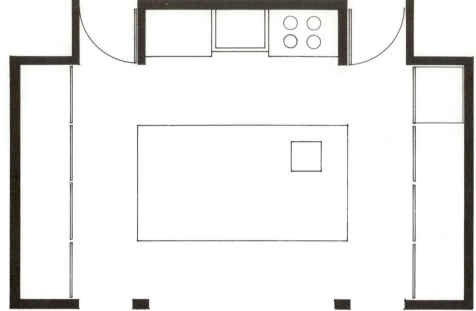

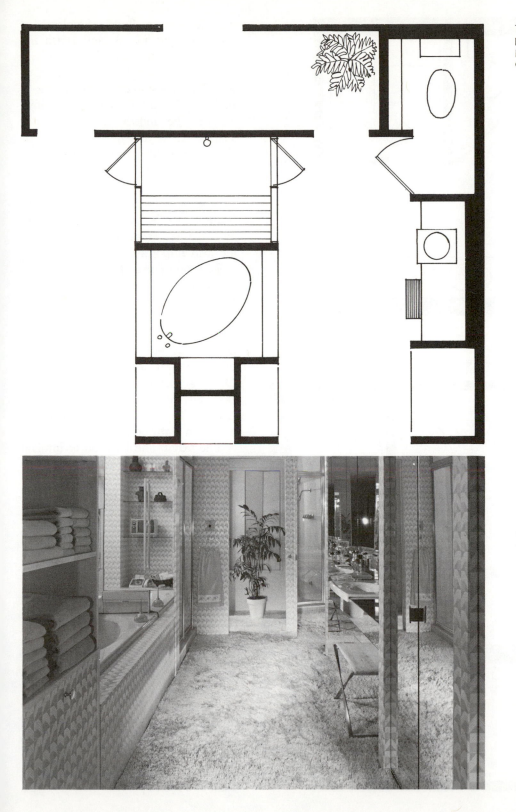

13–7   Luxurious bathroom (in plan, *above*) includes shag rug, plants, separate toilet and entrance areas.

13–8 Plans of typical segmented bathrooms.

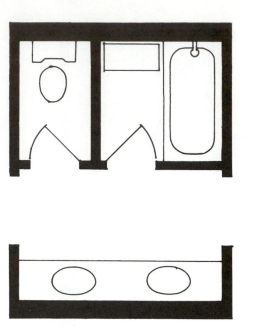

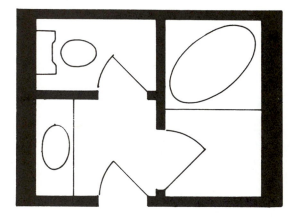

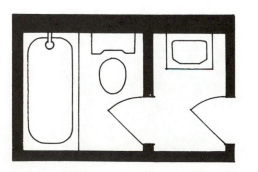

include marble floors, fireplaces, a chaise longue, plants, and lavish fixtures. Tubs are available in many shapes and capable of a variety of installations—sunken, raised, in a niche, against a wall, and so on. Showers can be in-tub or in variously shaped stalls having a curtain or sliding or folding doors of glass, fiberglass, or plastic.

The bathroom should be set apart, yet be readily accessible. Auxiliary heating may be useful. Pegs or hooks and counter space for small objects are also important.

Bathrooms may be segmented for family use (Fig. 13–8)—for example, the toilet, sink, and tub or shower may be located each in a separate area. Or a lavatory and a bathroom can be placed side by side, with a common entrance and a partition between. Often a bathroom of this kind may provide the necessary convenience without the considerable expense of a second bathroom.

The extent and location of integral storage space will be determined by the architect.

Homes for older persons (Fig. 13–9)—generally 65 years old or over (about 10 percent of the population today)—are much more attractive than in the past, and include space and equipment for greater activity. They often appear little different from a comfortable residential club. In planning this kind of environment, certain special needs should be considered. When possible, personal furnishings and mementos chosen by the occupants may be the basis of the design scheme. Chairs should be strong but light enough to be moved easily, and also easy to get out of—neither too low nor too soft. For the same reasons chair arms should be high enough to provide good leverage.

13–9   Room in a retirement home designed to meet special needs of older persons.

Rocking chairs are often preferred; they should be well balanced and placed so as to minimize the likelihood of anyone tripping over the rockers. Low tables should be avoided. Casters are helpful on beds that are placed against a wall. Beds should be firm and of a height so that they are easy to make up. Radio and television should be equipped with remote controls.

It is estimated that if the present rate of growth of vacation homes continues, there will be well over two million some time in the 1970's. Where the climate allows, vacation homes are often used at all seasons of the year.

13–10 Mountain ski house.
Below is one end of the room
seen through window wall
in exterior view.

13–11 Living room afloat; part of the family quarters of a vacation boat.

A mountain house (Fig. 13–10) designed for skiers needs a treatment different from a beach house or lakeside cottage. Similarly, a vacation home planned for a large family (Fig. 13–11) has little in common with one designed for a middle-aged couple. Low-cost minimal houses can be cleverly planned for maximum comfort and attractive appearance. Other houses, larger and better equipped, are frequently made into homes intended ultimately for retirement. Since relaxation is the essential aim in a vacation home, comfort and easy maintenance are prime virtues.

BIBLIOGRAPHY

AGAN, TESSIE, AND LUCHSINGER, ELAINE. *The House—Principles, Resources, Dynamics* (Lippincott, 1965). Practical and technical (though not design) aspects of planning a home.

ANDREW, WAYNE. *Architecture in America* (Atheneum, 1960). Introduction by Russell Lynes. Photographs—exteriors and interiors—of a wide variety of homes mainly from the early eighteenth century to 1959.

The Architectural Record Book of Vacation Houses (American Heritage Press, 1970). Selected by the editors of *The Architectural Record*. Many ideas and much information concerning vacation houses. Generously illustrated.

BERNIER, G., AND R. *European Decoration: Creative Contemporary Interiors* (Reynal, 1969). Excellent photographs of interiors in Europe, many built in the eighteenth century but in use now. Useful for decoration as well as design. From European art review *L'Oeil.*

Book of Holiday and Weekend Houses (St. Martin's Press, 1968). Photographs of vacation houses mostly from Western Europe, with a few from the United States.

GRANT, IAN, ed. *Great Interiors* (Dutton, 1967). Preface by Cecil Beaton. Photographs by Edwin Smith. Easy-to-follow evolution of interiors from 1650 to 1967, each period treated by a different authority. Lavishly illustrated with rarely seen photographs.

HEUSINKVELD, HELEN, AND MUSSON, N. *Buildings for the Elderly* (Reinhold, 1963). A good source with the emphasis on architecture.

JOHNSON, BETTY JANE. *Equipment for Modern Living* (Macmillan, 1965). How to choose and use household equipment. Well organized, specific, and good for reference.

KENNEDY, ROBERT WOODS. *The House and the Art of Its Domain* (Reinhold, 1953). Comprehensive and detailed coverage of all phases of living in a house in relation to design.

The Modern Room (Universe, 1967). Fine color photographs of rooms that represent solutions to household design problems.

MOODY, ELLA., ed. *Decorative Art in Modern Interiors* (Viking, 1971). Interiors, accessories, crafts, art objects, furniture. Photographs—some in color. A new issue each year showing developments for that period.

NELSON, GEORGE. *Living Spaces* (Whitney, 1952). Constructive suggestions on the best use of space for living.

NICOLSON, NIGEL. *Great Houses of the Western World* (Putnam, 1968). Photographs by Ian Graham. Covers the fifteenth to the nineteenth centuries, showing houses typical of the finest domestic architecture of thirteen countries, and illustrating the influence of one national style on another. Five of the thirty-six houses shown are in the United States; the others are distributed in twelve Western European countries.

PLUMB, BARBARA. *Young Designs in Living* (Viking, 1969). Photographs of interiors from the United States and Europe. Excellent.

PRAZ, MARIO. *An Illustrated History of Furnishing* (George Braziller, 1964). Four hundred paintings, drawings, and prints from unsigned, simple sketches by unknown artists to masterpieces by such artists as Vermeer, Hogarth, Dürer, and de Hooch depict a wide variety of interiors from Greece and Rome through Art Nouveau. Readable text is a running commentary on domestic environment.

Realities EDITORS. *Great Houses of Italy* (Putnam, 1968). Interesting text and photographs—not often seen—of exteriors, with excellent details. Exceptionally informative and detailed captions.

ROGERS, K. E. *The Modern House, U.S.A.* (Harper & Row, 1962) Comprehensive coverage of functional aspects, materials, methods of building, equipment, and appliances.

SAVAGE, GEORGE. *A Concise History of Interior Decoration* (Grosset and Dunlap, 1966). Interior decoration from Imperial Rome to the present. Very fine illustrations—many from private collections. Somewhat subjective, and the contemporary scene is oversimplified.

SITWELL, SACHEVERELL, ed. *Great Houses of Europe* (Putnam, 1961). Forty palaces, castles, villas, and halls —each described by an expert—in England, France, Spain, Portugal, Italy, Holland, Denmark, Sweden, Poland, Germany, and Austria. Excellent photographs.

TANGE, KENZO, AND KULTERMANN, UDO. *Kenzo Tange: Architecture and Urban Design* (Praeger, 1970). Comprehensive coverage of Tange's work, with each building illustrated by several photographs. Text is in English, German, and French.

WEISS, JOSEPH DOUGLAS. *Better Building for the Aged* (Hopkinson and Blake, 1969). Brief text with useful and specific information. Abundant illustrations, including floor plans and views of interiors, and exteriors.

WHITON, SHERRILL. *Elements of Interior Design and Decoration*, 3rd ed. (Lippincott, 1964). Comprehensive, full of facts. Includes complete history of residential interiors, primarily from decorating viewpoint. This edition has been updated to include some design.

WILLIAMS, HENRY LIONEL, AND OTTALIE K. *Great Houses of America* (Putnam, 1966). Thirty great houses and their furnishings built between the end of the seventeenth century and the late 1920's. Particularly interesting coverage of the mansions of the late nineteenth and early twentieth centuries. Many photographs, some in color.

It is likely that the next ten years will see as many changes in environment as have been introduced in the past one hundred. Today, new ideas succeed one another with such rapidity that products and techniques not yet out of the experimental stage, but reasonably certain of adoption by designers, will themselves soon be replaced. Forecast in 1961, photoelectric-cell door controllers, proximity and sound-activated switches, and atmosphere control are commonplace today, as are such things as wall units incorporating television, movies, and slide projection, and kitchens with largely automatic appliances accommodated to the use of frozen and disposable supplies.

Some forecasters of the house of the 1980's see it as strong on comfort, which seems to imply ever more technological innovations, although some yearn for a simple life divested of gadgets that are usually out of order. Most agree, however, that there will be more equipment—offering such things as quick and largely automatic food preparation and electronic home learning centers. Also predicted is wider use of plastics and lightweight metals.

NEW PRODUCTS

Some innovative trends are discernible in the design of products used in interiors. In carpeting, for example, a new generation of fibers will soon be introduced that, in conjunction with a special printing process, will make it possible to quickly dye and print carpet to order. Already being applied in the manufacture of some carpet are new and better methods of overcoming accumulation of static electricity; they will eventually be used in all new carpet. Carpets may also be used technologically: experiments have been carried out in which electrically conductive carpet provided the power to operate apparatus such as computers and tape machines, thus eliminating the need for conventional wiring.

New fast-action shuttleless looms are making possible more variety and better fabric at lower cost. Knit fabrics, which can be made more cheaply

EPILOGUE: THE FUTURE

than other fabrics, have not been as popular as they were expected to be; knits that are more practical than heretofore will be available soon. A fiber is being perfected by the use of which the elasticity of a woven or knit fabric can be predetermined. Certain woven or knit fabrics can now be heat-molded to the contours of a chair, either over a foam-padded frame or a solid molded form, to provide a permanent covering that will not stretch.

Although most new fire-resistant fibers are too expensive for general use, it is expected that costs will be reduced within a few years, and these fabrics will be in common use. One such fiber, Verel, is now being blended with other fibers with excellent results in both fabrics and carpets.

The decline in use of wood flooring is now being reversed. According to one authority, a unitized floor will replace joists, subfloor, and surface material. Units may be as large as 50 x 2 or 50 x 3 feet and will be installed at the stage at which joists are now put in place.

Expandable and inflatable furniture and module units are not very new, but the many new approaches to their design and use promise a much wider selection, probably at a lower cost. Good plastic furniture is still expensive, but new methods are being tested that are aimed at producing each piece in a single process (extrusion) that will permit mass-production and resultant lower costs.

Some predict that the kitchen of the future will consist only of essential appliances and storage in a movable unit. Others see free-standing modular appliances that can be used for different purposes in a basic kitchen area, or moved about and used in other parts of a house.

A demonstration house for the electronic age includes closed-circuit television for monitoring children at play; door locks with bedside controls so that all doors can be locked or checked from bed; push-button bathtub fixtures; a portable appliance center that does away with extension cords; outdoor patio heating; automatic temperature and atmosphere control; an intercom system that can communicate directly with local ser-

209

vices, such as fire, police, and school; and electric sewage disposal that treats waste water so it can be used for lawns and gardens.

Illuminating engineers have succeeded in producing light that provides full-spectrum illumination as well as ultraviolet radiation, which has germicidal properties. Some foresee light-conditioned buildings that may speed recuperation in hospitals, keep workers alert and productive, and, in general, make living more pleasant. Cordless electrical fixtures are being made, and soon to be available is a battery-operated lamp that will use standard light bulbs. An electrified track mounted on wall or ceiling gives more flexibility to an electrical system. Kinetic lighting, already used decoratively, is being developed as an aid in the treatment of disturbed children.

The use of infrared lamps for heating is becoming more widespread. The lamps heat directly by radiation —of the floor, objects, and people in a room—rather than indirectly, as in conventional systems, in which the air in a room is heated. This kind of heating is generally being used where large groups of people gather—gymnasiums, store entrances, indoor swimming pools, and so on.

A luminous-panel lamp is now available, adding a third variety to the point lighting of incandescent lamps and the line lighting of fluorescents. A single such lamp, as large as 2 x 4 feet, can produce green, blue, yellow, or white light and can be used with a dimmer control. Another version of this lamp, is a tape 1 inch wide and $\frac{1}{32}$ inch thick that can be made in lengths up to 150 feet. It has many commercial uses and has been used for unusual lighting effects.

Electrically conductive glass (p. 163) has many potentialities, and may eventually be used for both heat *and* light. The glass has exceptional strength, and its manufacturer foresees the time when buildings will be clad in it, so that the turn of a switch will transform a window wall into a glowing panel or into a panel that heats a room with radiant energy.

Another glass darkens, the brighter the light that falls on it; it can be controlled to produce any degree of light transmission, from completely transparent to opaque.

Almost all new buildings today have some degree of atmosphere and temperature control. Some new atmosphere control systems waste no heat. In a surprising number of cases, heat created by lighting and equipment, and the body heat of the occupants of a space are enough to heat it. Heat pumps use the differential in temperature between the ground and air to heat and cool. Heating and air conditioning from central plants is already a reality. Such plants provide chilled water, steam, or hot water to subscribers whose buildings may be miles from the plant.

Music is also becoming a more important part of interior environment. Automatic systems are available that can be installed so that they are virtually invisible. A remote-control unit permits listeners at up to fifty different locations to make selections and control the volume individually.[1]

According to forecasts, industrialized housing will be widespread before the end of this century. Complete factory-made houses, or those in which major parts are factory made, are now available and the trend

1. Boulton Electronics, New York, N.Y.

is toward much more and improved construction of this kind.

One of many examples of the use of plastics in "instant" building is the Bronson, Michigan, City Hall (32 x 60 feet), which was erected in fourteen hours and made largely of sandwiches of fiberglass, reinforced plastic, and urethane foam. Rigid urethane, a flotation material impervious to the elements, can be molded quickly for use in buildings. It can be made fire-retardant, is lightweight, and is not readily affected by temperature. Many kinds of plastic structures are being erected today; some will definitely survive the experimental stage.

NEW ATTITUDES

No interior designer can approach his work competently today without a knowledge of architectural trends and the presently projected ideas of urban planning.

As a result of United States–French cooperation in science and technology, a new city of 17,000 is being created today adjacent to the old Norman village of Vaudreuil, on the Seine, near Rouen. The city will be nonpolluting and, above all, flexible. Basic structures will be relatively permanent, but dividing elements (from walls to streets) will be changed to suit the people of the city. The site has been carefully selected for its natural beauty and recreation potentialities. A "lively social mix"—of architecture, space, activity, and people —is planned, and the public noise generated by this mix is anticipated as an asset. However, homes will be acoustically insulated from each other, and objectionable noise will be muffled or its source shifted to mini-

mize annoyance. Pedestrian convenience will have priority in the laying out of roads.

This is only one approach of many being tried. Paolo Soleri's super-cities would be built *up* on a scale that dwarfs the traditional skyscraper and are based on an ecology-conscious architecture. Whether or not these super-cities will rescue a society that he feels is suffering from "flat gigantism," the apprentice designer should be familiar with Soleri's ideas. Rather than architecture as it is known now, Moshe Safdie envisions an ideal architecture "machine" with which people could design their own buildings by simply pushing buttons. I. M. Pei has definite ideas about the intimate relationship between buildings and the surrounding air and trees in a space. Robert Venturi has written about and illustrated through his work some rather revolutionary ideas about architecture in environment. In Monte Carlo, a group called Archigram is building, for an estimated $7.2 million, a mechanized dome structure that is sunk into the ground and in which services will be controlled by a giant computer.

Even the accepted meaning of the term "architecture" is being reexamined. A contemporary nonarchitecture that, in a positive sense, "deals largely with such volatile things as process, choice, variety, transmutation and change" [2] may be necessary in order to cope with the rate and kind of change that can make buildings obsolete before they are actually in use.

Today, architects can design and engineers can build almost anything,

2. Ada Louise Huxtable, "The Endless Search," *New York Times*, October 3, 1971.

and people who are to use the resulting spaces are becoming more involved with and interested in their design. It is important for interior designers to familiarize themselves with the many and varied directions in which architecture is moving if they are to help people have the environments they want.

BIBLIOGRAPHY

ALEXANDER, CHRISTOPHER. *Notes on the Synthesis of Form* (Harvard Press, 1964). Advanced ideas result in an entirely new approach to design.

BANHAM, REYNER. *The Architecture of the Well-Tempered Environment* (University of Chicago Press, 1969). "Assesses the impact of environmental engineering on the design of buildings." Provocative, interesting, and informative.

GIEDION, SIGFRIED. *Mechanization Takes Command: A Contribution to Anonymous History* (Oxford University Press, 1970). The first comprehensive analysis of technological activities and their influence on people.

RUDOFSKY, BERNARD. *Architecture Without Architects* (Doubleday, 1964). An introduction to "non-pedigreed architecture." Photographs of universal structures, many primitive, from all over the world.

SAFDIE, MOSHE. *Beyond Habitat* (MIT Press, 1970). A personal statement by a unique and brilliant young architect.

STERN, ROBERT A. M. *New Directions in American Architecture* (George Braziller, 1969). The experimental work of the "third generation" of modern architects—written by one of them.

VENTURI, ROBERT. *Complexity and Contradiction in Architecture* (Museum of Modern Art, 1966). The controversial views of an architect who sees design virtues in prevailing twentieth-century American environment—such as the highway shopping strip—long held by others to be ugly and dehumanizing.

APPENDIX

APPENDIX

APPENDIX

PROFESSIONAL PRACTICE AND BUSINESS PROCEDURE

An apprentice designer who hopes to become a professional must have specialized training in interior architecture and construction, a background of basic and traditional design, and specific knowledge of the design and construction of furniture. He should be thoroughly familiar with all materials and products available, including their costs and sources. He should be able to deal smoothly with trade and labor sources, civic and government organizations, and architects and other professionals in the field of interior environment. He should be familiar with the systems approach to building, now being used in architecture and in interior design. This approach, by emphasizing mass-production methods, aims to lower the costs of good design.

The apprentice designer who would achieve professional status must also recognize the ethical foundations of the practice of interior design. His responsibility to a client is a serious one; when properly met it should result in an environment that he honestly considers good design and that satisfies the client. The designer must also operate on an ethical basis with his personnel and all trade sources. It is the further responsibility of the interior designer to press for high standards of design.

The basic division in the profession is that between residential and non-residential or "contract" interiors. Some designers do both kinds but specialize in one. Residential design includes everything from a one-room apartment to a mansion, a cabin to a deluxe apartment; nonresidential design covers offices, schools, public and institutional buildings, stores and shops, motels and hotels, theaters and restaurants.

The apprentice interior designer may enter the profession in various ways. He may work in a small firm, many of which offer design services free (as an adjunct to the sale of merchandise used in the design); in large shops (employing five to twenty or more interior designers); in department or furniture stores; or in architectural firms. In the foregoing, he will function as an interior designer. He may, however, also work in product design—developing furniture, lamps, fabrics, or other products for interiors—or teach interior design. Some interior designers combine two or more of these aspects.

A good client-designer relationship is vital to smooth execution of the designer's job. Learning to listen to what the client says and to truly understand what he means can contribute immeasurably to the achievement of that goal. Working with a client can be an educational experience, and what a client learns during the design process can, in turn, help to raise design standards in general.

The one absolute requisite in a presentation is clarity. Useful to this end are floor plans, elevations, detail drawings, perspectives, or isometric drawings or models—whatever is needed to make the design clear to the client, the contractor, and whoever will help carry it out.

Quantities of descriptive brochures and advertising are readily available to every level of interior designer, from the apprentice to the experienced professional. Although the purpose of this information is to sell, it can be valuable to the designer when he is ready, for example, to locate and purchase a specific rug or fabric, or a piece of furniture. However, the diverse sizes and shapes of sales catalogs make filing difficult, and the frequently poor organization and inadequate content make their use in general problematical. The seven-volume *Sweet's Interior Design File*, first made available in 1968, offers complete information on products used in interiors. It is distributed to design firms on the basis of the volume of their business, and for the present is used mainly by contract firms. The seven volumes of the *File* in its 1972 edition will cover the following: Volume 1, furniture; Volume 2, furniture, accessories, and art; Volume 3, coverings, finishes, fabrics, and a price list; Volume 4, lighting and building products and equipment; and Volumes 5–7, samples (such as cloth swatches) of products.

The financial aspects of interior design practice, including what clients, trade sources, or the business community will expect of the designer, are covered clearly in *A Guide to Business Principles and Practices for Interior Designers* (Whitney Publications Inc., New York). The book is organized so that it can be useful to a student or apprentice as well as to a practicing designer. It shows how to analyze and solve operational problems and provides forms essential to the systemizing, control, and integration of business operations with design work.

Trade and Generic Names of Principal Carpet Fibers

TRADE NAME	GENERIC TYPE	PRODUCER
ACE Nylon	nylon	Allied Chemical Corp.
Acrilan, Acrilan 2000	acrylic	Monsanto Textiles Division
Anavor	polyester	Dow Badische Company
Anso	nylon	Allied Chemical Corp.
Antron, Antron 11	nylon	E. I. duPont de Nemours & Company Inc.
Avlin	polyester	American Viscose, division F.M.C.
Cadon	nylon,	Monsanto Textiles Division
Caprolan	nylon	Allied Chemical Corp.
Celanese nylon	nylon	Fiber Industries Inc., division Celanese
Coloray	rayon	Courtaulds North America Inc.
Creslan	acrylic	American Cyanamid Company
Cumuloft	nylon	Monsanto Textiles Division
Dacron	polyester	E. I. duPont de Nemours & Company Inc.
Durel	olefin	Fiber Industries Inc., division Celanese
Dynel	modacrylic	Union Carbide Corp.
Encron	polyester	American Enka Corp.
Enkalite	polyester	American Enka Corp.
Enkaloft	nylon	American Enka Corp.
Enkalure	nylon	American Enka Corp.
Enka Nylon	nylon	American Enka Corp.
Fibro	rayon	Courtaulds North America Inc.
501 Nylon	nylon	E. I. duPont de Nemours & Company Inc.
Fortrel, Fortrel ECF	polyester	Fiber Industries Inc., division Celanese
Herculon	olefin	Hercules Inc.
Kodel	polyester	Eastman Chemical Products Inc.
Marvess, Marvess CG	olefin	Phillips Fibers Corp.
Orlon	acrylic	E. I. duPont de Nemours & Company Inc.
Patlon	olefin	Patchogue Plymouth
Phillips 66 Nylon	nylon	Phillips Fibers Corp.
Polycrest	olefin	Uniroyal
Polyloom	olefin	Chevron Chemical Company
Shareen	nylon	Courtaulds North America Inc.
Source	biconstituent nylon/acrylic	Allied Chemical Corp.
Spectrodye	nylon	American Enka Corp.
Super Stuff	polyester	Beaunit Corp.
Tough Stuff	polyester	Beaunit Corp.
Trevira	polyester	Hystron Fibers Inc.
Vectra	olefin	Enjay Fibers and Laminates Company
Verel	modacrylic	Eastman Chemical Products Inc.
Vivana	nylon	Dow Badische Company
Vycron	polyester	Beaunit Corp.
Weatherbright	modacrylic/acrylic	Dow Badische Company
Weathertuff	olefin	Bigelow Sanford (trade name for Durel)
Wellene	polyester	Wellman Inc.
Wellon Nylon 6/6	nylon	Wellman Inc.
Zefchrome	acrylic	Dow Badische Company
Zefran	acrylic	Dow Badische Company
Zefran CR 4	synergistic acrylic/nylon	Dow Badische Company
Zefstat	anti-static yarn	Dow Badische Company

ARCHITECTURAL TERMINOLOGY

Italicized terms are themselves defined in this glossary.

Abutment The masonry structure that receives the lateral thrust of an arch.

Arabesque A scroll pattern in which flowers, foliage, fruits, geometrical forms, and sometimes human and animal figures are intertwined.

Arcade A line of arches (supported on piers or columns) used to form covered passageways.

Arch A curved structure that spans an opening. The curve may be part of a circle, or flattened or pointed at the top.

Architrave The lowest division of an entablature. It rests on the capital of a column and corresponds to a *lintel*.

Baluster A slender, turned column of a series that support a handrail; together, a balustrade.

Base The lower portion of any structure or architectural feature.

Bay window A window or windows projecting from a room, forming a recess on the interior.

Bead molding A small, round molding sometimes raised only slightly from the surrounding surface, sometimes projecting so as to have a semicircular cross-section.

Bolection molding A molding at the edge of a panel that projects beyond the surface of the rest of the frame.

Bracket A projecting member that supports a weight, traditionally with a scroll form. Called modillions or consoles when used in a traditional cornice.

Broken pediment A *pediment* that is broken or open at its peak, usually enclosing some kind of ornament.

Buttress A masonry structure positioned against walls at intervals to add stability.

Capital The crowning feature of a *column* or *pilaster*.

Cartouche A scroll-like ornament, usually oval in shape, used decoratively.

Casement window A window that is hinged on one side.

Chimneypiece See *mantel.*

Colonnade A series of regularly spaced *columns*.

Column A vertical support, usually composed of *base*, shaft (cylindrical), and a spreading *capital*.

Corinthian One of the *orders* of Greek architecture.

Cornice The crowning member of an architectural composition, most frequently the horizontal *moldings* at the top of a wall.

Cove As part of a cornice, a concave curve between wall and ceiling.

Dado The lower part of the wall of a room if treated differently from the upper part or separated from it by an ornamental *molding*.

Dentil A small oblong block, used regularly spaced to decorate moldings —often in *cornices*.

Doric The simplest *order* of Greek architecture.

Dormer window A window having its own gable, which projects from a sloping roof.

Double-hung window A window having movable upper and lower sections, the upper one sliding behind the lower.

Elevation A drawing of a vertical (nonperspective) plane, usually done to scale.

Engaged column A column attached to a wall.

Entablature The upper part of a building (usually the façade); in the Greek *orders* it includes the *cornice*, *frieze*, and *architrave*.

Entasis A curving outward in the outline of a *column's* shaft.

Façade The face or front of a building.

Fluting Vertical channeling on the shaft of a *column* or *pilaster*.

Frieze The middle division of the classical Greek *entablature*.

Ionic One of the *orders* of Greek architecture.

Keystone The central, uppermost stone of an *arch*.

Lintel A horizontal member spanning an opening.

Loggia A roofed gallery open at a side or sides.

Lozenge A diamond-shaped *motif* used in architectural decoration.

Mantel The facing around the opening of a fireplace, including the part that projects from the wall.

Medallion A round or oval form, used as a frame, often containing a classic head or an ornamental *motif* painted or in relief.

Molding A narrow surface (applied to a wall), projecting or recessed, plain or ornamented, that is continuous.

Motif A central or repeated figure in a design.

Module A basic unit of which the dimensions of the major parts of a building or work are multiples.

Niche A recess in a wall.

Order In classic architecture a style embodied in the characteristic design of *column*.

Patio An interior court open to the sky.

Pediment In classical architecture, a triangular, low-pitched gable formed by the ends of the roof and the *cornice*.

Perspective A means of rendering three-dimensional objects on a flat surface.

Pier A large support of stone that differs from a *column* in that its cross-section is square or polygonal.

Pilaster A flat, rectangular feature using the design of a column and projecting about one-sixth of its breadth from a wall.

Plan A drawing or diagram showing in horizontal section the arrangement of a structure.

Portico A porch or vestibule with a roof supported on at least one side by *columns*.

Reeding A series of parallel lines in relief—the reverse of *fluting*.

Rustication Stone masonry in which the joints are recessed and squared and the face of the stone is rough.

Spandrel The roughly triangular space formed by the outer curve of an *arch* and a rectangle that encloses the arch.

Soffit The underside of an architectural member.

Vault An arched roof or ceiling of masonry.

Wainscot A wooden facing for an interior wall, frequently paneled.

FURNITURE TERMINOLOGY

Apron A flat piece filling the space bounded by the upper portions of the legs of a table or chair and the table top or chair bottom.

Armoire A free-standing closet, usually furnished with a lock.

Banquette A bench, usually long and often built into or placed against the wall.

Bergère An armchair with upholstered back, seat, and sides, with an exposed decorative wood frame.

Boiserie Wainscoting.

Bombé Bulging or rounded.

Butterfly table Small, folding table, with drop leaves, supported by wing brackets shaped somewhat like butterfly wings.

Cabriole A furniture leg that curves in from the foot and terminates at the top with an outward curve.

Candelabra A large branched candlestick (also Candelabrum).

Chaise longue A long couchlike chair that came into use in the late seventeenth century.

Chinoiserie Chinese designs adapted for use in France to decorate wallpapers, textiles, wood panels, and furniture.

Comb-back Windsor A Windsor chair with a high back set like a comb into a broad top rail.

Commode A chest of drawers developed from low chests that opened from the top.

Console A bracket or shelf fastened to a wall, or a table designed to be used against a wall.

Credenza A cabinet that combines shelves and doors, used for storage.

Drop-leaf table A table with hinged leaves that can be folded down.

Escritoire A writing table or secretary.

Fauteuil Upholstered armchair, similar to a *bergère* but with open space between arms and seat.

Fiddleback A chair back with a center *splat* shaped like a fiddle.

Finial An ornamental top-piece used on furniture or lamps.

Gallery A raised or fretted rim of wood or metal used on edge at the top of a piece of furniture.

Gate-leg A table with leaves that are supported by legs that can be folded back against the frame.

Gimp A narrow, flat decorative cloth trim for upholstered furniture and curtains.

Girandole A *candelabra* with arms that usually form a circle.

Highboy A chest of drawers mounted on a stand or legs.

Hutch A cabinet with doors and, often, shelves above.

Inlay Design in a wood surface made by setting in pieces of contrasting wood, metal, or other materials level with the surface.

Kneehole desk A desk with a flat top and drawers at either end, with a space between for the knees.

Ladder-back chair Chair with horizontal slats between upright supports.

Love seat A small upholstered sofa made to seat two.

Lowboy Small table with drawers, similar to the lower part of a *highboy*.

Lustre A chandelier made of crystal.

Mount Ornamental or functional metalwork, usually handles or pulls.

Ormolu An alloy of copper and other metals that resembles gold.

Ottoman Backless, cushioned seat also used as a footrest.

Papier-maché A material made of paper pulp mixed with oil, glue, or resin and that can be molded.

Pedestal table Table supported by a center base rather than four legs.

Pediment A form similar to the triangular gable at the ends of Greek temples, used over doorways, mantels, and to top high pieces of furniture.

Pembroke table Small rectangular table with drop leaves, rounded or squared, with square, tapered legs and a drawer.

Piecrust table Table with a raised, scalloped, or fluted edge around its top.

Refectory A long, narrow table of a design similar to those used in monastery dining halls.

Repoussé Relief metalwork formed by beating from its underside.

Reproduction A copy that is a close imitation or a duplication of an original design.

Restoration The restoring or putting back into original condition of anything that has been damaged by use or age.

Side chair An armless chair with a small seat.

Splat The thin, flat piece of wood used in the back of a chair.

Stretcher Brace connecting the legs of furniture.

Swag A decorative device simulating a festoon of fabric, flowers, leaves, or fruit in a draped form.

Tester The wooden canopy on a four-poster bed.

Tilt-top table A table with a top hinged to the base so the top can be turned to stand upright.

Tole Painted and decorated metal—usually tin.

Torchère A large floor candleholder or candelabra.

Veneer A thin layer of choice wood bonded to a heavier, usually inferior, piece.

FIXTURES AND APPLIANCES

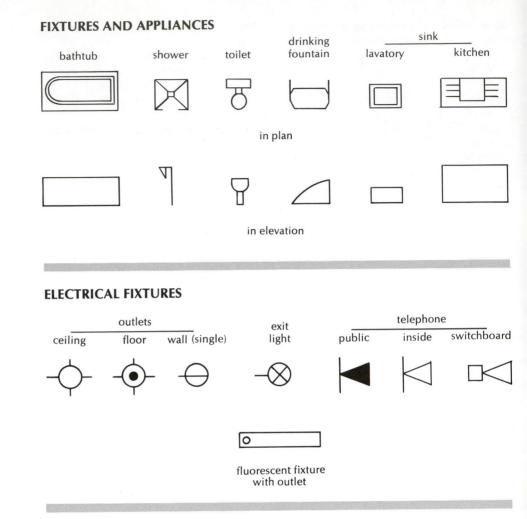

bathtub   shower   toilet   drinking fountain   sink — lavatory kitchen

in plan

in elevation

ELECTRICAL FIXTURES

outlets — ceiling floor wall (single)   exit light   telephone — public inside switchboard

fluorescent fixture
with outlet

VENTILATING AND AIR CONDITIONING APPARATUS

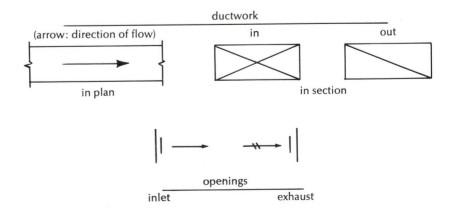

ductwork

(arrow: direction of flow)   in   out

in plan   in section

openings
inlet   exhaust

INDEX

INDEX

ILLUSTRATION SOURCES

All drawings except those in the appendix are by Richard Coats.

Chapter 1 Fig. 1, Museum of the City of New York, New York. Fig. 2, Photograph by Byron. Museum of the City of New York, New York. The Byron Collection. Fig. 3, Julius Shulman. Fig. 4, John T. Hill.

Chapter 2 Fig. 2, "The Interior of the Pantheon," Giovanni Paolo Panini. National Gallery of Art, Washington, D.C. The Samuel H. Kress Collection. Fig. 3, Alinari-Art Reference Bureau. Fig. 4, G. Savage, *A Concise History of Interior Decoration*, Thames & Hudson, London. Fig. 5, *Connaissance des Arts*—R. Guillemot. Fig. 6, Ramsay. Fig. 7, *Connaissance des Arts*—R. Bonnefoy. Fig. 8, The Metropolitan Museum of Art, New York. Rogers Fund, 1911. Fig. 9, Courtesy of The Cooper-Hewitt Museum of Decorative Arts and Design, Smithsonian Institution, Washington, D.C. Fig. 10, *left* The Metropolitan Museum of Art, New York. The Sylmaris Collection. Gift of George Coe Graves, 1930; *right* The Metropolitan Museum of Art, New York. Gift of Louis J. Bowry, 1933; *opposite page* The Metropolitan Museum of Art, New York. Gift of Henrietta McCready Bagg and Ida McCready Wilson in memory of their mother, Ann McCready, 1936. Fig. 11, R. B. Fleming & Co. Fig. 12, The Metropolitan Museum of Art, New York. Rogers Fund, 1911. Fig. 13, Cooper-Hewitt Museum of Decorative Arts and Design, Smithsonian Institution, Washington, D.C. Fig. 14, H. M. Wingler, *Bauhaus*, Verlag Gebr. Rasch & Co. Fig. 16, Ezra Stoller Associates, Inc. Fig. 17, Mies van der Rohe, *The German Pavilion*, International Exposition, Barcelona, Spain, 1929. Fig. 18, Trans World Airlines. Fig. 19, Courtesy of The Museum of Modern Art, New York. Fig. 20, Ezra Stoller Associates, Inc. Fig. 21, Cervin Robinson. Fig. 22, Bill Hedrich Blessing.

Chapter 3 Fig. 1, The Solomon R. Guggenheim Museum, New York. Fig. 2, American Museum of Natural History, New York. Fig. 3, John T. Hill. Fig. 4, *top* American Museum of Natural History; *bottom* Wolcott and Carlson. Fig. 5, John T. Hill. Fig. 6, G. Savage, *A Concise History of Interior Decoration*, Thames & Hudson, London. Fig. 7, Jack Lowery and Associates, Inc. Fig. 8, McMillen, Inc. Fig. 10, Louis Reens. Fig. 12, Robert Perron. Fig. 13, Jon Naar. Fig. 14, Geoffry Clements. Courtesy of M. J. Alexander. Fig. 15, McMillen, Inc. Fig. 16, John T. Hill.

Chapter 5 Fig. 1, L. Jarmin Roach, AID. Fig. 2, Geoffry Clements. Courtesy of M. J. Alexander, AID. Fig. 3, Courtesy of Faber Birren. Fig. 4, L. Jarmin Roach, AID. Fig. 5, Joseph Braswell Associates, Inc. Fig. 6, McMillen, Inc. Courtesy of House & Garden. Fig. 7, Joseph Braswell Associates, Inc. Fig. 8, Joseph Braswell Associates, Inc. Fig. 9, McMillen, Inc. Fig. 10, Joseph Braswell Associates, Inc. Fig. 11, John T. Hill. Fig. 12, McMillen, Inc. Fig. 13, Robert Perron. Fig. 14, Fortrel polyester contract carpets. Fig. 15, Joseph Braswell Associates, Inc. Fig. 16, Norman McGrath.

Chapter 6 Fig. 1, Marble Institute of America. Fig. 2, John T. Hill. Fig. 3, *top right* Cities Service (Fritz Henle); *top left* Helen Faye; *bottom right* Design Photographers International. Fig. 5, General Electric Company. Fig. 6, *top left* Jack Shaw, NSID of Walter W. Scarborough, Inc.; *top right* Atelier International, Ltd.; *bottom* Ford Foundation (Ezra Stoller). Fig. 7, *top (all photos)* Habitat; *bottom left* Lighting Associates, Inc.; *bottom right (all photos)* Atelier International, Ltd. Fig. 8, *left page* Michael Saphier, NSID; *opposite page* General Electric Company. Fig. 9, *top* John T. Hill; *bottom* Ken Nahan, NSID. Fig. 10, Ezra Stoller. Courtesy of Eleanor Le Maire. Fig. 11, General Electric Company. Fig. 12, John T. Hill. Fig. 13, General Electric Company. Fig. 14, *top* Charlotte Finn,

NSID; *bottom* General Electric Company. Fig. 15, Walton Stowell, NSID. Fig. 16, Robert Perron.

Chapter 7 Fig. 1, McMillen, Inc. Courtesy of House & Garden. Fig. 3, Angelo Donghia for Burge-Donghia, Inc. Fig. 4, Jack Lowery and Associates, Inc. Fig. 5, Melanie Kahane, FAID. Fig. 6, Jon Naar. Courtesy of Ward Bennett. Fig. 7, Allied Chemical Corporation (Caprolan Nylon) and Regal Rugs. Fig. 8, V'soske/Lord & Adams. Fig. 9, Ezra Stoller Associates, Inc. Fig. 10, Melanie Kahane, FAID.

Chapter 8 Fig. 1, *top left* Carol D. Sigel, NSID; *top right* Philip Graf Wallpapers, Inc.; *bottom right* Melanie Kahane, FAID. Fig. 2, T. Miles Gray, NSID. Fig. 4, *left page* Angelo Donghia for Burge-Donghia, Inc.; *right page* Window Shade Manufacturers Association. Fig. 5, *opposite page* Window Shade Manufacturers Association; *right page, top* General Electric Co.; *right page, bottom* McMillen, Inc. Fig. 6, *top* McMillen, Inc.; *bottom left* John T. Hill; *bottom right* Robert Perron. Fig. 7, *top left* Louis Reens. Courtesy of Elizabeth Draper, Inc.; *top center* Jack Lowery and Associates, Inc.; *top right* Jerry Law, AID; *bottom* Beverly Reitz.

Chapter 9 Fig. 1, Window Shade Manufacturers Association/Design by Charles S. Gelber, AID. Fig. 2, McMillen, Inc. Fig. 3, McMillen, Inc. Fig. 4, Allied Chemical Corporation. Fig. 5, Owens-Corning Fiberglas Corporation. Fig. 6, Syroco.

Chapter 10 Fig. 1, Thedlow, Inc. Figs. 2 and 3, John T. Hill. Fig. 4, Marble Institute of America. Fig. 5, David Williams. Fig. 6, Alexander Georges. Courtesy of Valerian Rybar, AID. Fig. 7, *right page, bottom* Bloomingdales; *right page, top* Directional; *opposite page* Directional.

Chapter 11 Fig. 1, Louis H. Frohman. Courtesy of the Shaker Museum, New York. Fig. 2, Thedlow, Inc. Fig. 3, *right*

Thonet Industries; *left* Joseph Braswell Associates, Inc. Fig. 4, Mies van der Rohe, *Armchair*, 1926. The Museum of Modern Art, New York. Gift of Edgar Kaufmann, Jr., Fund. Fig. 5, Mies van der Rohe, *Lounge Chair* (Barcelona chair), 1929. Gift of Knoll Associates, Inc., U.S.A. Fig. 6, Atelier International, Ltd. Fig. 7, Bonet, Durchan, and Ferrari-Hardoy, *Lounge Chair*, 1938. Gift of Edgar Kaufmann, Jr., Fund. Fig. 8, Charles Eames, *Dining Chair*, 1946. The Museum of Modern Art, New York. Gift of the Herman Miller Furniture Co. Fig. 9, Bertoia, *Armchair*, 1952. The Museum of Modern Art, New York. Gift of Knoll Associates, Inc., U.S.A. Fig. 10, Saarinen, *Armchair*, 1957. The Museum of Modern Art, New York. Gift of Knoll Associates, Inc., U.S.A. Fig. 11, Jens Risom Design. Fig. 12, Atelier International, Ltd. Fig. 13, *top* Ginsburg and Levy, Inc.; *bottom* The Metropolitan Museum of Art, New York. Gift of J. Pierpont Morgan, 1906; *opposite page, top and bottom left* Atelier International, Ltd.; *opposite page, bottom right*, Harvey Probber, Inc. Fig. 14, Window Shade Manufacturers Association. Fig. 15, McMillen, Inc. Fig. 16, Directional "CityScape" Collection designed by Paul Evans.

Chapter 12 Fig. 1, *opposite* Angelo Donghia for Burge-Donghia, Inc.; *top left* Robert Perron; *top right* John T. Hill. Fig. 2, John T. Hill. Fig. 3, Courtesy of Eleanor Pepper.

Chapter 13 Fig. 1, Ruiko Yoshida. Fig. 2, Ezra Stoller Associates, Inc. Fig. 3, *top* McMillen, Inc.; *bottom* Jack Lowery and Associates, Inc. Fig. 4, *right* Gordon Reeve Gould; *left* John T. Hill. Fig. 5, General Electric Company. Fig. 6, Jon Naar. Courtesy of Benjamin Baldwin. Fig. 7, Allied Chemical Corporation. Fig. 9, Dan Acito, NSID. Fig. 10, Melvin Dwork Associates, Inc. Fig. 11, Henry End Associates.

Appendix Common Architectural Symbols, Harbrace.